Curso Completo de Inglés
Teach Yourself English

Habla Inglés desde la segundo lección.
Nivel Dos avanzado.
Aprenda Inglés sin profesor hoy.

Dr. Yeral E. Ogando

Curso Completo de Inglés – Nivel Dos
© 2016 por Dr. Yeral E. Ogando
Publicado: Christian Translation LLC
Impreso en los EE.UU
Diseño de Portada por SAL media

ISBN 13: 978-1-946249-99-9
ISBN 10: 1-946249-99-8

1. Language Learning - Aprender un Idioma.
2. English Language – Idioma Inglés

DEDICACIÓN:

Éste libro está dedicado a la Única y duradera persona que siempre ha estado ahí para mí, sin importar cuán terco soy:
DIOS

Sin Ti mi Dios, nada soy. Gracias por tu misericordia e inmerecedora Gracia.

AGRADECIMIENTOS:

Gracias a Dios por permitir que mi sueño se hiciera realidad y por darme fuerzas cuando sentí ganas de renunciar.

De no haber sido por el apoyo que he recibido a lo largo del camino de parte de éstas increíbles y sorprendentes personas, no estaría donde estoy hoy.

Gracias a mi editora, Sharon A. Lavy y a los "Diseñadores de la Portada", SAL media por haber hecho un gran trabajo ayudándome con esta obra.

Elizabeth McAchren por su excelente colaboración e ideas durante la creación de este segundo libro de la serie. Coleman Clarke y Kathryn Ganime-Leech por su increíble trabajo en el audio.

Éste ha sido una muy larga jornada para mi familia, pero la recompensa es digna. Gracias a mi padre, Héctor y a mis hijas, Yeiris y Tiffany por permanecer a mi lado a través de éste viaje. Saben que les amo.

God bless you all
Dios les bendiga

Dr. Yeral E. Ogando
www.aprendeis.com

DEDICACIÓN:

Éste libro está dedicado a la Única y duradera persona que siempre ha estado ahí para mí, sin importar cuán terco soy:
DIOS

Sin Ti mi Dios, nada soy. Gracias por tu misericordia e inmerecedora Gracia.

AGRADECIMIENTOS:

Gracias a Dios por permitir que mi sueño se hiciera realidad y por darme fuerzas cuando sentí ganas de renunciar.

De no haber sido por el apoyo que he recibido a lo largo del camino de parte de éstas increíbles y sorprendentes personas, no estaría donde estoy hoy.

Gracias a mi editora, Sharon A. Lavy y a los "Diseñadores de la Portada", SAL media por haber hecho un gran trabajo ayudándome con esta obra.

Elizabeth McAchren por su excelente colaboración e ideas durante la creación de este segundo libro de la serie. Coleman Clarke y Kathryn Ganime-Leech por su increíble trabajo en el audio.

Éste ha sido una muy larga jornada para mi familia, pero la recompensa es digna. Gracias a mi padre, Héctor y a mis hijas, Yeiris y Tiffany por permanecer a mi lado a través de éste viaje. Saben que les amo.

God bless you all
Dios les bendiga

Dr. Yeral E. Ogando
www.aprendeis.com

TABLE OF CONTENTS

Introducción 7

SÍMBOLOS Y ABREVIACIONES 8

Looking after the house and the children –
Cuidando la casa y nos niños 13

Getting ready for the wedding – Preparandose
para la boda 31

The robbery – El robo 53

Going for a walk – Dar un paseo 75

Getting sick - Enfermandose 91

Five star hotel – Hotel cinco estrella 111

Conversational Level Two – Nivel de
Conversación Dos 133

Level Two Tests – Examenes del Nivel Dos
....149

Verb list – Lista de verbos 157

Grammar Summary 161

Answers to exercises – Respuestas de los
ejercicios 164

Answers to Level Two Tests – Respuesta de
los Examenes del Nivel Dos 170

Conclusión 174

BONO GRATIS 175

Introducción

He publicado este método para que puedan aprender inglés en forma rápida y eficaz.

Les pido que dediquen 20 minutos dirios al estudio del inglés sin interrupción, para que puedan concentrarse y digerir el contenido de esta obra. Uno de los desafíos más grande del aprendizaje es ser una persona Autodidacta, en otras palabras, que aprende por cuenta propia. Se requiere mucha disciplina y dedicación en el estudio para poder lograr un buen aprendizaje. Estudiar una hora completa cada día puede hacerlos sentirse aburridos o cansados rápidamente, esta es la razón por la que les recomiendo un mínimo de 20 minutos y un máximo de 40 minutos al día para mejor aprendizaje. De este modo podrán lograr mejores resultados.

Les deseo Buena suerte en este increíble viaje al mundo del aprendizaje del idioma inglés, y recuerden, *"Hablen sin vergüenza"*

Dr. Yeral E. Ogando
www.aprendeis.com

SÍMBOLOS Y ABREVIACIONES

Audio: Indica que se necesita el Audio MP3 para esta sección. No olviden que cada oración o palabra en inglés está disponible en audio MP3.

Dialogo: Indica dialogo o texto de lectura.

Gramática: Indica la gramática o explicación de la estructura del idioma

Ejercicios: Indica las secciones para ejercicios y prácticas.

Prólogo

Muchas personas creen que *"Aprender Inglés"* es una tarea muy difícil, de modo que se pasan la vida con el deseo de Aprender Inglés, pero nunca se deciden por el miedo o tabú que se les han inculcado, que el Inglés es muy difícil de aprender.

Estoy completamente de acuerdo con las personas que dicen que es difícil Aprender Inglés, puesto que nunca han tenido el método adecuado o la enseñanza correcta para aprenderlo. En otras palabras, siempre será difícil Aprender Inglés sino se tiene la herramienta adecuada.

No olviden que no todo el que enseña, sabe enseñar. Existen muchos profesores y muchos métodos para aprender, sin embargo, la mayoría de ellos no abordan la forma correcta para el aprendizaje del estudiante. Este método ya les ha demostrado en el primer nivel, lo sencillo que es poder "hablar Inglés" en poco tiempo. Después de mas de 10 años de experiencia y vivenciando la forma rápida del aprendizaje de mis estudiantes, pongo en sus manos este tesoro.

Les he demostrado lo fácil que es aprender este idioma usando mi método. Ya ustedes están hablando inglés, ahora necesitan desarrollar sus habilidades y hablar más fluido. No tienen que esperar meses y años, como ya han visto, podrán ver lo rápido que avanzarán en su nivel de conversación.

Este curso es para enseñarles la forma correcta de Aprender Inglés, reconociendo los patrones y formas de hablar; aun podrán aprender un poco más de español en este increíble viaje.

Siempre recomiendo a mis alumnos que estudien un mínimo de 20 minutos y un máximo de 40 minutos al dia. Esto les permitirá aprovechar al máximo su aprendizaje y a la vez a mantener la mente activa en el idioma. No traten de estudiar varias horas un dia a la semana, porque se fatigarán y aburrirán, no llegando a sacarle provecho al aprendizaje. Es mejor un poco con calidad que mucho sin efectividad.

Recuerden que los sonidos y pronunciaciones deberán ser escuchados y aprendidos en el transcurso del curso, usando la herramienta del audio para cada sección.

PASOS PARA USAR ESTE LIBRO Y SACARLE EL MEJOR PROVECHO

Asegúrense de **DESCARGAR** el Audio del libro con las instrucciones encontradas en la página "**BONO GRATIS**" este método no tiene la pronunciación marcada o habla de la pronunciación, es **IMPERATIVO** descargar el audio para poder aprender la pronunciación correcta del inglés.

1. Ve a la página de "**BONO GRATIS**" y descarga el audio del libro.

2. Lee la conversación del libro, escuchando la pronunciación directamente del audio. Asegúrate de captar la pronunciación y practicarla.

3. Lee y aprende las nuevas palabras, frases y expresiones encontradas en la sección "*New Words*" y "*Phrases and Expressions*".

4. Ahora debes concentrarte en la gramática de la lección. Esta es la parte más importante y lo que te permitirá hablar correctamente. Presta mucha atención a cada explicación y en especial a la estructura de las palabras. Recuerda que necesitas el audio para las oraciones o ejemplos encontrados en todo el libro. Nunca pases a otra sección o lección sin antes dominar completamente la gramática.

5. Ahora necesitas regresar al inicio de la lección y escuchar una vez más las conversaciones hasta que puedas comprenderlas bien y asimilar la estructura.

6. Repasa las nuevas palabras, frases y expresiones hasta que las aprendas bien y asegúrate de lograr la pronunciación como la del audio. El desafío más grande que tienes es dominar la pronunciación y pronunciar como la voz nativa del

audio MP3.

7. Es tiempo de realizar los ejercicios. Asegúrate de llenar y practicar cada ejercicio. Los mismos medirán tu comprensión de la gramática de la lección. Una vez llenes tus ejercicios, revísalos una y otra vez, y cuando ya estés seguro. Entonces, podrás ver las respuestas al final del libro, solo para comparar y asegurarte de que lo hiciste bien. No hagas trampa.

8. Ya terminaste la lección. Felicidades. Ahora debes regresar al inicio de la lección una vez más y repasarla por completo, como si fuera la primera vez. Si viste que los conceptos expresados los entendiste bien y los manejaste a la perfección, es porque estás listo para pasar a la siguiente lección. De lo contrario, entonces, deberás seguir el repaso de la lección hasta que la domines a la perfección.

Lesson 1

Looking after the house and the children – Cuidando la casa y nos niños

Conversation 1

Doorbell: [*Ding dong*]

Karen: Hello?

Cindy: Hi. My name is Cindy.

Karen: It's nice to meet you.

Cindy: Nice to meet you, too. I'm looking for volunteers for the Neighborhood Watch program.

Karen: Yes?

Cindy: Well, we need someone to keep an eye on activity on this street between the hours of 9 a.m. and 12 p.m.

Karen: I'm sorry. I'm very busy during those hours.

Cindy: Oh, really? Since you don't work, I thought—

Karen: What?

Cindy: Well, you're just a housewife, right?

Karen: *Just* a housewife?

Cindy: Yes, I mean, you don't have a job, do you?

Karen: I don't have a job, but I work. I pick up, dust, sweep, and mop. I do the laundry, fix lunch, and I have to finish any extra projects—shopping, sewing, etc.—before my kids come home from school.

13

Cindy: Right, but I'm sure you can listen to what's happening in the street and check to see if everything's okay.

Karen: If I hear anything, I will check on it. But most of the time I listen to music to help me keep moving.

Cindy: Do you have to listen to music all the time?

Karen: Look, I think you'd better find someone else to help you, okay?

Conversation 2

Waiter: Good afternoon. Can I take your order?

Customer: Well, I'm waiting for a friend, but I don't have much time, so . . . do you have a seniors menu?

Waiter: Yes, one moment, please. . . . Here you are.

Customer: Thank you. . . . I'd like the stuffed mushrooms to start with.

Waiter: Would you like anything to drink?

Customer: Yes. Is the cider pretty good?

Waiter: Delicious. All of our customers rave about it.

Customer: Sounds great.

[15 minutes later]

Waiter: How was your appetizer?

Customer: Delicious, thank you.

Waiter: Would you like to order the main dish?

Customer: Well, I'd like to wait for my friend, but—tell you what—why don't you bring my dessert first?

Waiter: That's fine. What would you like? Our apple tart is quite popular.

Customer: Well, today, I think I'd like the bread pudding.

Waiter: Great. Would you like some coffee with that?

Customer: Sure.

[15 minutes later]

Waiter: How was your dessert?

Customer: Wonderful. You know what, I don't think my friend is coming, so why don't you bring me the bill.

Waiter: Sure. If you would like, I can prepare a box of food to go. The special today is veal parmigiana, and the roast beef is also excellent.

Customer: No, I've had enough, thank you.

Conversation 3

Diana: You wouldn't believe what your children did today! Jason wrote on the walls. At least he used chalk, and it's not permanent. Then Carrie got into the shortening and got it all over the house. Look! You can see her footprints on the floor. They are always making more work for me. And you too! How many times do I have to tell you to leave your shoes by the door?

Shawn: But I'm on my way out, darling. I'm going to see your mother—to see how she's doing.

Diana: Can't you find the snake out back and kill it first?

Shawn: I'll do it later.

Diana: Well, don't take too long. Give my regards to mother.

Shawn: Okay, dear.

Opal: Hi, Shawn. What's the matter? Is Diana in one of her moods?

Shawn: You can say that again. She's really stressed out with her new job. She sends her regards, by the way.

Opal: Thanks. New job?

Shawn: You know, she's selling bags and purses.

Opal: Bags and purses? Is that a lot of work?

Shawn: I guess it's hard to get started, and she already has her hands full with the kids.

Opal: Hmmm. Well, I've already got a visitor, but that's okay. Come on in to the living room. I'd like you to meet my friend, Darice. This is my son-in-law, Shawn.

Shawn: Hi, Darice, it's nice to meet you.

Darice: Nice to meet you, too, Shawn. You're a handsome young man.

Shawn: Thank you [chuckling].

Opal: If you're hungry, you can check the fridge.

Shawn: Okay, thanks! . . . Yum, is this shrimp cocktail?

Opal: Oh, that's no good. I made that on Sunday. There's some steak on the bottom shelf.

Darice: So what do you do, Shawn?

Shawn: I'm a writer.

Darice: Where do you work?

Shawn: At the Herald.

Darice: Really? Do you wear khakis to work?

Shawn: Yes. We dress pretty casual.

Darice: Oh, that's too bad. Young men never dress up anymore. You would look so nice in a suit.

Shawn: Thank you. I do wear a suit when I have an important interview.

Darice: Really? Who do you interview?

Shawn: Oh, sometimes the mayor or some of the wealthier women who are involved in a lot of social activities. That's when I really dress up.

Darice: Yes, we appreciate formality.

Shawn: Do you like to participate in society, Darice?

Darice: Well, yes, I host some fundraising events, and I volunteer at the local school.

Shawn: Really?

Darice: Yes, I read to the children.

Shawn: That's nice. Actually, I guess I'd better be going. I should help Diana get the kids to bed. They like at least three stories at bedtime.

Opal: Okay. She still watches soap operas, doesn't she? Tell her I said no more soap operas. If she wants to have time for extra jobs, she has to get the housework done before the kids get home from school.

Shawn: Why don't you call her? I think she'd take it better from you.

Opal: All right. First thing tomorrow. Make sure she gets to bed early, too. No TV.

New words – Nuevas palabras
Address – dirección

Phone number – número telefónico
Darling - querido (a)
Regards – saludos / recuerdos
Announcer – locutor / anunciador
Channel - canal
Cruise - crucero
The Caribbean – El caribe
Island – isla
Through – a través
*If – si
*All of - todo
Passport control – control de pasaporte / verificación de pasaporte
Port - puerto
Soap – jabón
Sun - sol
Swimming pool - piscina
Travel agency – agencia de viajes
Travel agent – agente de viajes
Bill – factura / cuenta
Birthday - cumpleaños
Bread - pan
Carrot - zanahoria
Cheesecake – bizcocho de queso
Chopstick – palitos chinos
Century - siglo
Main course – plato principal
First course – plato de entrada
Dessert - postre
Duck - pato
Fork - tenedor
French fries – papas fritas

Hand - mano
Lettuce - lechuga
Melon - melón
Menu - menú
Mushrooms – hongos / champiñones
Onion - cebolla
Peas - guisantes
Poison - veneno
Pudding - pudin
Sauce - salsa
Shrimp – camarones (es singular y plural a la vez, no se le agrega s)
Shrimp cocktail – coctel de camarones
Snail - caracol
Snake - serpiente
Spoon - cuchara
Steak – filete / bistec
Veal – ternera
Volunteers - voluntarios

Remarks:

If – si condicional:
If you want to eat, you have to work. – Si quieres comer, tienes que trabajar.

All of – todo: da la idea del todo sobre una cantidad.

All of you – todos ustedes (de un grupo).

All of the boys – todos los chicos (de un grupo)

Phrases and Expressions - Frases y expresiones

A Friend of mine – un amigo mío
Cheers – salud *(cuando se brinda)*

How do you do? - ¿Cómo te va?

I'd like you to meet my friend – me gustaría que conocieras a mi amiga.

We'd like you to meet our friends- nos gustaría que conocieras a nuestros amigos.

Nice to meet you – encantado de conocerte

Pleased to meet you – es un placer conocerte

Look – mira *(usada como comodín al hablar)*

To send your regards – enviar recuerdos / saludos

You know – tú sabes

All the time – todo el tiempo

Congratulations - felicidades

Can I take your order? - ¿Puedo tomar su orden?

House specialty – especialidad de la casa

Could you help me, please? - ¿Podrías ayudarme, por favor?

Happy birthday – feliz cumpleaños

How old are you? - ¿Qué edad tienes?

To have your hands full – tener las manos llenas

Nowadays – hoy en día

Neighborhood Watch program – programa de vigilancia del vecindario.

To keep an eye on activity - vigilar la actividades

To rave about it – alardear a cerca de algo

Grammar – Gramática

Como les había comentado, en este segundo nivel tendremos menos explicaciones y más acción, debido a que la base para todo son las lecciones pasadas. Vamos a incrementar nuestros conocimientos y a iniciar este segundo nivel.

Nivel Dos

Tag questions – Coletilla interrogativa

Se usa cuando el hablante espera que quien escucha confirme o niegue lo que está diciendo, o espera que el oyente este de acuerdo con lo dicho. Cuando tenemos una declaración negativa, el "*tag question*" estará en afirmativo y cuando tenemos una declaración afirmativa, el "*tag question*" estará en negativo. Recuerden, siempre será lo inverso al igual que en español.

Decimos ¿te comiste la comida? *¿No es verdad?* O ¿no te comiste la comida? *¿Verdad?* A esto nos referimos con "tag question", veamos en inglés ahora.

I am clever, *aren't* I? – soy inteligente. ¿No es así?
Yes, you are. – Si, lo eres.
Yes, you are clever – Si, tú eres inteligente.

You aren't crazy, *are you*? – tú no estás loco. ¿O sí?
No, I am not. – No, no lo estoy.
No, I am not crazy – No, no estoy loco.

He is smart, *isn't he*? – él es inteligente. ¿No es así?
Yes, he is – Si, lo es.
Yes, he is clever – Si, él es inteligente.

She isn't young, *is she*? – ella no es joven. ¿O sí?
No, she isn't – No, no lo es.
No, she isn't young – No, ella no es joven.

It is good, *isn't it*? – Es bueno. ¿No es así?
Yes, it is – Si lo es.
Yes, it is good. – Si, es bueno.

We are rich, **aren't we?** – Somos ricos. ¿No es verdad?

Yes, we are. – Si, lo somos.

Yes, we are rich – Si, somos ricos.

You are foolish, **aren't you?** – Eres tonto. ¿No es así?

Yes, I am – Si, lo soy.

Yes, I am foolish – Si, soy tonto.

They aren't fat, **are they?** – Ellas no son gordas. ¿O sí?

No, they aren't – No, no lo son.

No, they aren't fat – No, ellas no son gordas.

Presten atención al "tag question" I am, siempre será "aren't I? cuando la declaración sea afirmativa. Pero cuando la declaración sea negativa, se usa la conjugación normal.

I am not crazy. **Am I?** – No estoy loco, ¿O sí?

No, you're not – No, no lo eres.

No, you're not crazy – No, no estás loco.

Would (wouldn't) like – Gustaría (no)

En lecciones anteriores ya vimos el uso del "would like"; repasemos un poco el "would like".

Questions – preguntas

Whom would I like to see? - ¿A quién me gustaría ver?

What would you like to see? - ¿Qué te gustaría ver?

Why would you like to see it? - ¿Por qué te gustaría

verlo?

Where would you like to see it? - ¿Dónde te gustaría verlo?

When would you like to see it? - ¿Cuándo le gustaría verlo?

Which would he like to see? - ¿Cuál le gustaría ver?

How would she like to see it? - ¿Cómo le gustaría verlo?

How long would we like to see it? - ¿Por cuánto tiempo nos gustaría verlo?

How much would you like to pay? - ¿Cuánto les gustaría pagar?

How many would they like to buy? - ¿Cuántos les gustaría comprar?

Affirmative answers – Respuestas afirmativas

I'd like (I + would) ... – me gustaría...

You'd like (you + would) ... – te gustaría / le gustaría...

He'd like (he + would)... – le gustaría...

She'd like (she + would) ... – le gustaría...

It'd like (it + would) ... – le gustaría...

We'd like (we + would) ... – nos gustaría...

You'd like (you + would) ... – les gustaría...

They'd like (they + would) ... – les gustaría...

Negative answers – Respuestas negativas

I wouldn't like... - no me gustaría...

You wouldn't like... - no te gustaría...

He wouldn't like... - no le gustaría...

She wouldn't like... - no le gustaría...

It wouldn't like... - no le gustaría...

We wouldn't like... - no nos gustaría...
You wouldn't like... - no les gustaría...
They wouldn't like... - no les gustaría...

Would you like to eat with me today? - ¿te gustaría almorzar conmigo hoy?
Yes, I would – Sí.
Yes, I'd like to eat with you today – Sí, me gustaría comer contigo hoy.
No, I wouldn't – No.
No, I wouldn't like to eat with you today – No, no me gustaría comer contigo hoy.

Recuerden,
Respondemos "wouldn't" para cosas que no queremos hacer. Pero cuando alguien nos ofrece algo, entonces, decimos "No, thank you".
Would you like some cake? – ¿te gustaría algo de bizcocho?
No, thank you – No, gracias.
No, I wouldn't, thanks. I'd prefer some juice – No, gracias. Preferiría algo de jugo.

Adjectives – Adjetivos
*Alone - solo
Same – igual / mismo
Duty-free – libre de impuestos
Excited - emocionado
Main – principal / primordial
Pleasant -agradable
Boiled - hervido
Broiled – asado a la parrilla

Different - diferente
Enough - suficiente
Fried - frito
Medium – medio cocido
Rare – casi crudo
Roasted - asado
Special - especial
Well-done – bien cocido (referente a comida)
*Alone: lo usamos solo cuando nos referimos a la persona "I am alone – estoy solo".
Pero decimos:
I just want to talk to you - solo quiero hablar contigo.
I only want to talk to you – solamente quiero hablar contigo.
Presten mucha atención y no se confundan.

Adverbs – Adverbios
Ago – hace (solo se usa en el pasado)
The day before yesterday – Antes de ayer
Hard – duro, difícil
Last – último / pasado
Never - nunca
Normally - normalmente
Rarely - raramente
Really – realmente
Immediately - inmediatamente
Also - también
Anywhere – en cualquier lugar
Certainly - ciertamente
Instead (of) – en vez de
Somewhere – en algún lugar

Always - siempre
Usually - usualmente
Often – a menudo
Sometimes – algunas veces

New regular verbs – Nuevos verbos regulares

To call – called - llamar
To look after – looked after - cuidar
To pick up – picked up - recoger
To cash – cashed – cambiar *(dinero)*
To cook – cooked - cocinar
To dance – danced - bailar
To fish – fished - pescar
To listen to – listened to – escuchar a
To report – reported - reportar
To smoke – smoked - fumar
To start – started – iniciar / comenzar
To talk – talked - hablar
To want – wanted - querer
To work – worked - trabajar
To land – landed - aterrizar
To use – used - usar
To board – boarded - abordar
To check in – checked in - registrarse
To kiss – kissed - besar
To like – liked - gustar
To mail – mailed – enviar por correo
To open – opened - abrir
To rain – rained - llover
To rent – rented - rentar
To rest – rested - descansar

New irregular verbs – Nuevos verbos irregulares
To forget – forgot - olvidar
To get – got – conseguir / obtener
To go dancing – went dancing – salir a bailar
To send – sent - enviar
To get up – got up - levantarse
To make – made – hacer - fabricar
To put on – put on – ponerse *(ropas)*
To get to – got to – llegar a *(un lugar o destino)*
To give – gave - dar
To go in – went in – entrar *(cuando la persona está afuera y va a entrar)*
To come in – came in – entrar *(cuando la persona está dentro y quiere que entres)*
To take off – took off – despegar (un avión)
To fly – flew - volar
To run – ran - correr
To swim – swam - nadar
To wear – wore – usar / llevar puesto
To bring – brought - traer
To eat out – ate out – comer fuera *(un restaurante, etc)*

📝 **Exercises – Ejercicios**

Exercise 1.1: Write the tag question. Use the correct pronoun to rename the subject of the first sentence. If the sentence uses the verb *to be*, use the verb *to be*. If it contains a helping verb, use the same helping verb. If it uses some other verb, use the verb *do*. Keep the verb tense the same, but remember to change from negative to affirmative or from affirmative to negative.

He's smart, _isn't he?_

My parents didn't call me, _did they?_

You love her, _don't you?_

1. She's a happy baby, _____

2. It didn't rain, _____

3. You like chocolate, _____

4. Mom is really busy, _____

5. Dad wasn't sleeping, _____
6. You can't rest with all that noise,

_____

7. Mom doesn't know you're sick,

_____

8. You can walk, _____

9. Mr. Walker isn't here, _____

10. You go running every day, _____

Exercise 1.2: Underline the logical sentence. Remember, the condition should begin with *if.*

Example: If you want to get a job, you need to dress formally. / If you need to dress formally, you want to get a job.

1. If she wants to get her work done, she shouldn't watch soap operas. / If she shouldn't watch soap operas, she wants to get her work done.
2. If they can deliver newspapers, they want to make extra money. / If they want to make extra money, they can deliver newspapers.
3. If you call me first, Mom lets you go to the movies. / If Mom lets you go to the movies, call me first!
4. If you finish your work early, we can go out to eat! / If we can go out to eat, you finish your work early.
5. If I can't do the laundry, it rains. / If it rains, I can't do the laundry.

Exercise 1.3: Write the correct question word.
Example: When are visiting hours? Right now. _Whom_ would you like to see?

1. "I'd like some pens. _____
2. ___ would you like to buy?" "Five, please."

3. "Let's go to the movies. _____ would you like to see?"
"An action movie, of course!"
4. "I want to go see my mom. _____ would you like to see her?"
"On Sunday."
5. "I need to see the schedule. _____ do you need to see it?"
"I want to see who is talking first—my boss or me."

6.   "Let's go out. _____ do you want to go?"

"Let's go to the park downtown!"

Lesson 2

Getting ready for the wedding – Preparandose para la boda

Conversation 1

Haidresser: Come right in, honey. So you're getting married in a couple hours? How do you feel?

Bride: Oh, nervous, excited, you know, like everyone.

Haidresser: Yeah. I remember my wedding day. I thought life would be so perfect. But it's just work, work, work.

Bride: Really?

Haidresser: Well, you know, before you're married, he comes to see you, takes you out to eat, and gives you presents. After you're married, he comes home to eat, takes you to the grocery store, and gives you dirty laundry.

Bride: Ah, right. What do you do to keep the love alive?

Haidresser: Well, I guess I don't do much. I just try to keep him alive. Haha. Okay, we're almost done with the hair. Do you want to see it? Now, for your makeup: do you want a dramatic look or something more subtle?

Bride: I'd like it natural, please.

Haidresser: Okay. And for your lipstick? I recommend red for those pictures.

Bride: Um, I guess red would be nice.

Haidresser: Good. Would you like your nails red, too?

Bride: Sure.

Haidresser: So, where are you going for your honeymoon?

Bride: I don't know. It's a surprise!

Haidresser: Oh, that could be nice. The groom doesn't like camping, does he?

The wedding

There was the bridge, two left turns, the eternal traffic light, and a right turn into the parking lot. Frank could hardly believe the day was finally here. As he walked into the church, there was a quick flash of white and a door closed. Christie would cry if he saw her before the wedding. She was very traditional. He knocked on the closed door. "How are things going in there?" he asked. There was no answer. He slipped a note under the door and continued down the hall to the men's restroom.

Behind the door, Christie read the note and cried. After years of dreaming of her wedding day, there were so many unexpected emotions. It wasn't all flowers and romance. She was making a big commitment! From now on, she would plan meals, wash dishes, pick up socks, dust, sweep, and mop— and she would do this after getting out of work. It wouldn't be easy. Could she do it? Could she work all day and still be nice to Frank at the end of the day?

She read the note again. She was promising loyalty

to the man she loved, to the man who bought her
flowers and chocolates, to the man who taught her
Scrabble and golf. Frank was an expert at basketball
and poetry. She couldn't imagine life without him.
She dried her tears, reapplied her makeup, and
arranged the train of her dress behind her.

As she walked up to the door, she could just see
Frank by the altar. He was so handsome—and kind.
The usher opened the door. Her father took her arm,
wiping tears from his own eyes. Everyone was crying,
apparently, even the flower girl, who became nervous
and ran to her mother. Christie laughed and walked
down the aisle toward Frank. Her father gave her to
her husband. The pianist played terribly. He had two
jobs and no time to practice. But the bride and groom
didn't notice. They said their vows, exchanged rings,
and kissed, all the time promising eternal love with
their eyes.

When they turned around, the saw their parents
crying and smiling. It would be difficult, but they
would make each other happy. And even if they
weren't always happy—because Christie knew that
sometimes they wouldn't feel happy—they would still
love each other. She could learn a new type of love:
one that didn't depend on chocolates and flowers. Her
love would create sunshine on rainy days. She chose
to face the future with hope instead of fear.

Frank looked at his wife. He was completely
happy. She was so beautiful, so radiant. They
practically flew out of the auditorium. Everyone
congratulated them and promised to help them
through the future months and years. It was a perfect

day, a day to remember in hard times. Now they just had to find a job.

Conversation 2

Clerk: Welcome to Legend Lodge. We're so glad you chose to stay with us! Let's see. Do you have a reservation?

Frank: Yes, for five nights.

Clerk: Hmmm. Well, it looks like your reservation is for tomorrow night.

Frank: No, there must be some mistake. I made it from Saturday to Wednesday.

Clerk: I'm sorry. You are currently booked from Sunday to Thursday, but we'll see if we can change it. . . . You're in luck! We have a free room tonight, but it's not the bridal suite. How about we put you in the forest room tonight and tomorrow you can change to the bridal suite?

Frank: Is there an extra charge?

Clerk: No, if you are only staying five nights, the cost remains the same.

Frank: Great!

Clerk: Would you like some supper? There's a buffet in the dining room to your right. It's complementary—included in the price of the room. Go right in and see what's there while I process your card.

Frank: Looks delicious!

Clerk: Fantastic. Here's your key. Your room is straight down the hall. Would you like some help with your bags?

Frank: No, we're fine, thanks.
Clerk: Call me if you need anything!

New words – Nuevas palabras
Barber shop – barbería / peluquería
Bridge - puente
Bus stop – estación de autobús
Chemistry - química
Class - clase
Corner – esquina
Hall – corredor / pasillo
Driver – conductor / chofer
Hairdresser - estilista
Jail – cárcel
Jeweler - joyero
Left - izquierda
Right - derecha
Library – bliblioteca
Math / Mathematics – matemáticas
Mistake - error
Museum - museo
Parking lot – parqueo / estacionamiento
Professor – profesor
Real estate agency – agencia de bienes raíces
Receptionist – recepcionista
Road – carretera / calle
Subway – subterráneo / metro
Supermarket – supermercado
Traffic light – semáforo
University - universidad
Area – área
Band – banda / grupo

Best man – padrino (de una boda)
Bride – novia (de la boda)
Bridesmaid – damas de honor
Future - futuro
Groom – novio (de la boda)
Guest - invitado
Honeymoon – luna de miel
Meter - metro
Reception – recepción
Studio – estudio
Surprise - sorpresa
Truck – camión
Usher – ujier
Wedding - boda
Answer – respuesta
Application – solicitud
Appointment – cita
Business – negocio
Company - compañía
Form – forma
Manager – gerente
Personnel – personal
Question - pregunta
Salary – salario
Word - palabra
Worker - trabajador
Aunt – tía
High school – escuela secundaria / bachillerato
Life - vida
Tourist – turista
Uncle - tío
Writer - escritor**Phrases and Expressions - Frases y**

expresiones

To be right – estar en lo cierto (correcto) / tener la razón

To be wrong – estar equivocado

Could you tell me …? - ¿Podrías decirme…?

Could you tell us…? - ¿podrías decirnos?

Do you mind if…? - ¿te importaría si…?

To make a mistake – cometer un error / meter la pata

Sure - seguro

To take the bus – tomar el autobús *(abordarlo)*

To take the plane – tomar al avión *(abordarlo)*

I hope so – eso espero

I think so – eso pienso / creo

I guess so – eso supongo

I hope not – espero que no

I guess not – supongo que no

I don't think so – no lo creo

To take a vacation – tomar vacaciones

To come right in – entrar de inmediato *(cuando la persona está dentro y te invita a entrar)*

To go right in – entrar de inmediato *(cuando la persona está afuera y te indica que entres)*

Good to see you – es bueno verte / encantado de verte

What can I do for you? - ¿Qué puedo hacer por ti? ¿En qué te puedo servir?

What can we do for you? - ¿Qué podemos hacer por ti?

To get a job – conseguir un trabajo / empleo.

📖 Grammar – Gramática

Aprendemos un poco más sobre la forma cortés de pedir o preguntar las cosas. Veamos las preguntas y oraciones normales y como las convertimos en formal o cortes.

"Could you tell... May I ask...".

How old *are you*? - ¿Qué edad tienes?

Could you tell me how old *you are*? - ¿podrías decirme que edad tienes?

May I ask how old *you are*? - ¿puedo preguntar qué edad tienes?

Ustedes pueden ver como la simple pregunta "how old are you?" se convierte en una pregunta cortes con tan solo usar **"could you tell... May I ask...".**
Presten mucha atención a la estructura, porque cuando usamos esta forma de cortesía, ya la pregunta original no está como pregunta. Veamos lo que les estoy explicando.

Decimos "How old *are you*?" Recuerdan que "*Are you*" es la forma para preguntas del verbo "to be".
Pero cuando usamos "May I ask how old *you are*?", estamos diciendo "*You are*" no en forma de pregunta, sino como afirmación, porque ya el "May I ask" o "Could you tell..." hace la forma de pregunta. ¿Comprenden la idea? Vamos a seguir practicando el modelo.
Excuse me; could you tell us what time it is? -

¿excuseme, podrías decirnos que hora es?

May I ask what time it is, please? - ¿podrías decirnos que hora es, por favor?

May I ask if I made any mistakes? - ¿puedo preguntar si cometí algún error?

Could you tell me if I made any mistakes? - ¿podrías decirme si cometí algún error?

Ustedes pueden convertir cualquier pregunta en forma cortes. Recuerden, cuando usamos el "may", la pregunta es más suave y cortes. En cambio, cuando usamos "could" la pregunta tiene un tono un poco más fuerte en comparación con el "may".

Modal verb *Can* / *Could* – Verbo modal *Can* / *Could.*

Recuerden que ya vimos el uso del "Can" en lecciones pasadas, de modo que solo daremos un repaso y nos concentraremos en "could".

I can talk now – puedo hablar ahora.

I can't talk now – no puedo hablar ahora.

Can I speak now? - ¿Puedo hablar ahora?

Yes, you can. – Si, puedes.

No, no you can't. – No, no puedes.

Ahora vamos a aprender el uso del "could". Tiene dos usos diferentes dependiendo de la conversación y el contexto.

Could – podría

I can speak now – puedo hablar ahora.

I could speak now – podría hablar ahora.

I can fly the plane – puedo volar el avión.
I could fly the plane – podría volar el avión.

I can't sing opera – no puedo cantar ópera.
I couldn't sing opera – no podría cantar ópera.
Could you sing opera? - ¿podrías cantar ópera?
Yes, I could. – sí, podría.
Yes, I could sing opera – si, podría cantar ópera.
No, I couldn't – no, no podría.
No, I couldn't sing opera – no, no podría cantar ópera.

Recuerden, el patrón es el mismo. Nunca se usa un verbo en infinitivo cuando usamos "could".
Could you sing then? - ¿podrías volar entonces?
No, I couldn't fly anymore – no, no podría volar más.

Could – pasado de "can"

Este es el segundo uso del "could", el cual es el pasado de can y tenemos que tomar muy en cuenta esto, dependiendo el contexto o la oración. Veamos.
Could you talk to the teacher yesterday? - ¿pudiste hablar con el profesor ayer?
Yes, I could. – Si, pude.
Yes, I could talk to the teacher yesterday – Si, pude hablar con el profesor ayer.
No, I couldn't. – No, no pude.
No, I couldn't tak to the teacher yesterday – No, no pude hablar con el profesor ayer.

Como pueden ver, siempre que usamos "could" para el pasado el verbo permanece en presente; es como cuando aprendimos el "did". No lo olviden.

What happened to you yesterday? - ¿Qué te pasó ayer?

I couldn't swim, I had cramps – No pude nadar, tenía calambres.

I couldn't come yesterday, because I was sick. – No, pude venir ayer porque estaba enfermo.

El concepto está claro, solo tienen que comenzar a usarlo con los otros conocimientos ya adquiridos. Si se ponen a analizar, ustedes tienen un nivel de inglés casi equivalente a un año de universidad. Ya pueden hablar en casi todos los tiempos. Sigamos nuestro aprendizaje.

Auxiliary verb "used to" – Verbo auxiliar"used to" – solía.

Usamos el "used to" para cosas que solían pasar regularmente en el pasado, pero ya no ocurren más.

I used to cook – solía cocinar *o* acostumbraba a cocinar *(pero ya no cocino más).*

I used to go to church every Sunday – acostumbraba ir a la iglesia todos los domingos *(pero ya no más).*

She used to play the piano – ella solía tocar el piano *(pero ya no más).*

Para preguntas y respuestas negativas, como es el pasado, usamos el "***did / didn't***". Veamos.

41

Did you use to play the piano? - ¿acostumbrabas tocar el piano?

Yes, I used to. – Sí, solía.

Yes, I did. – Sí.

No, I didn't use to. – No, no solía.

No, I didn't. – No.

Tenemos la opción de contestar de dos formas, con el "did" o con el "*used to*".

Recuerden que cuando usamos el "*did*" el verbo debe ir en presente, es por esto que usamos "*use to*" en preguntas y respuestas negativas. Continuemos practicando.

Did you use to cook for your husband? - ¿acostumbrabas cocinar para tu esposo?

Yes, I used to. – Si, solía.

Yes, I did. – Si.

Yes, I used to cook for my husband. – Si, solía cocinar para mi esposo.

No, I didn't use to. – No, no solía.

No, I didn't. – No.

No, I didn't use to cook for my husband. –No, no solía cocinar para mi esposo.

Did you use to play cards? - ¿acostumbrabas jugar cartas?

Yes, I used to play cards – Si, acostumbraba jugar cartas.

No, I didn't use to play cards – No, no acostumbraba jugar cartas.

Algunas veces cuando usamos el negativo,

podemos reemplazar el "didn't" por el "never". Cuando usamos "never" el "used to" tiene que ir en pasado.

I didn't use to sing at home – No acostumbraba a cantar en casa.

I never used to sing at home – nunca acostumbraba a cantar en casa.

Did you use to smoke? - ¿acostumbrabas a fumar?

I never used to smoke – nunca acostumbraba a fumar.

I didn't use to smoke – no acostumbraba a fumar.

Siempre que no se use el "did", entonces el "used to" deberá estar en pasado. No lo olviden.

I always used to smoke – yo siempre acostumbraba a fumar.

I used to work from time to time – acostumbraba a trabajar de tiempo en tiempo.

I used to flirt a lot – solía coquetear mucho.

New regular verbs – Nuevos verbos regulares
To look for – looked for – buscar
To turn – turned – girar / doblar
To hope – hoped – esperar *(de esperanza)*
To intend – intended – tener la intención
To answer – answered - responder
To apply for – applied for - solicitar
To ask – asked – pedir o preguntar
To earn – earned - ganar
To expect – expected - esperar
To fill out – filled out – llenar *(formulario)*
To type – typed – digitar / escribir en la

computadora

To bore – bored - aburrirse

To die – died - morir

To learn – learned - aprender

New irregular verbs – Nuevos verbos irregulares

To be born – was / were born - nacer

To become – became - convertirse

To hit – hit - golpear

To say – said - decir

To pay – paid - pagar

To sit down – sat down - sentarse

To understand – understood - entender

To find – found – encontrar / buscar

To get married – got married - casarse

To get on – got on – montarse / subirse *(en un vehículo)*

To get off – got off – desmontarse / bajarse *(de un vehículo)*

To tell – told – decir / contar

Prepositions – Preposiciones

Across – a través de / de un lado a otro

Across the Street – al otro lado de la calle *(esto es, cruzando la calle)*

Along – a lo largo

Walk along the street – camine a lo largo de la calle

Down – abajo – hacia abajo

Turn down the Street – gire hacia abajo en la calle

Over – sobre / encima

We have to go over the bridge – tenemos que pasar por encima del puente

Up – arriba / hacia arriba
Let's go up – vamos a subir
On top of – en la cima de / en la parte superior
They are on top of the mountain – ellos están encima de la montaña. *(Es decir, en la parte superior, en el pico de la montaña)*
Straight ahead – al frente / todo derecho
Continue straight ahead and then turn right at the first traffic light – continúa todo derecho y entonces gira a la derecha en el semáforo.

Estas preposiciones las usamos usualmente cuando estamos dando dirección e indicaciones.

Adjectives – Adjetivos
Left – izquierda
Turn left at the next corner – gira a la izquierda en la siguiente esquina.
Right – derecha
Don't turn right – no gires a la derecha
Boring - aburrido
Closed - cerrado
Enormous - enorme
Fantastic - fantástico
High - alto
Lucky - suertudo
Old-fashioned – pasado de moda
Open - abierto
Square – plaza / manda
Sure - seguro
Total - total
Careful – cuidadoso / cuidado

Careless - descuidado
Fast - rápido
Immediate - inmediato
Loud – alto (de volumen)
Low – bajito / bajo
Hard – duro / rudo
Noisy - ruidoso
Present – presente / regalo
Quick – rápido / ágil
Slow – lento / despacio
Soft – suave / blando
Famous - famoso
Following – siguiente

Adverbs – Adverbios
A Little – un poco
Maybe – tal vez / quizás / puede ser
Yet - todavía
Anymore – nunca más / ya
Badly – gravemente / mal
Carelessly – descuidadamente
Carefully - cuidadosamente
Happily - felizmente
Loudly – altísimo
Noisily - ruidosamente
Quickly – rápidamente / ágilmente
Quietly - tranquilamente
Sadly – tristemente
Slowly – lentamente
Softly – suavemente
Terribly – terriblemente

Como pueden ver, para formar la terminación "mente" en inglés, solo tenemos que agregar "ly" al adjetivo y lo convertimos en adverbio. Veamos.

He is a bad pilot – él es un mal piloto

He flies the plane badly – el vuela el avión malamente.

You are careful – eres cuidadoso

You speak carefully – tú hablas cuidadosamente

You are a careless driver – eres un conductor descuidado

You drive carelessly – conduces descuidadamente

We need an inmediate answer – necesitamos una respuesta inmediata

Answer immediately – responde inmediatamente

He's a quick mechanic – él es un mecánico rápido

He works quicky – él trabaja rápidamente

The music is terrible because they sing terribly – la música es terrible porque ellos cantan terriblemente

Recuerden que con los adjetivos que terminan en "y", se cambia por una "i" y entonces se le agrega "ly". Los adjetivos que terminan en "le", quitamos l "e" y le agregamos la "ly".

Estos son irregulares y nunca cambian.
Fast – fast
She is a fast driver – ella es una conductora rápida
She drives fast – ella conduce rápido

*Good – well
I am a good teacher – soy un buen profesor
I teach well – yo enseño bien.

Hard –hard
You are a hard worker – eres un arduo trabajador
You work so hard - trabajas muy duro

Presten mucha atención, especialmente a "good – well". Nunca pueden decir "I speak good", eso sería como decir "Yo hablar bueno". Y ya establecimos que la era de los cavernículas pasó. Tenemos que decir
I speak well – yo hablo bien
They learn well – ellas aprenden bien
I am a good learner – soy un buen aprendiz

The word "so" – La palabra "so"
So puede variar su significado dependiendo del contexto; veamos.

So – muy / tan
It is *so* good, isn't it? – es tan bueno, ¿no es así?
They are *so* beautiful, aren't they? – ellas son muy hermosas, ¿no es así?
I am *so* happy – estoy tan feliz

So – por motivo de eso / así que / de modo que
I listened to the radio *because* I didn't like the TV shows – Escuchaba la radio porque no me gustaban los programas de TV.

I didn't like the TV shows, *so* I listened to the radio. – No me gustaban los programas de TV, así que escuché la radio.

I changed the channel *because* I didn't like the movie – cambié el canal porque no me gustaba la película.

I didn't like the movie, *so* I changed the channel. – No me gustaba la película, sí que cambié de canal.

So – Si, No

Are they saying something? I think *so*... ¿están ellos diciendo algo? Creo que si...

Sería lo mismo que contestar.

Yes, I think they are saying something - Sí, creo que ellos están diciendo algo.

Is she doing something? I don't think *so* - ¿está haciendo algo? Creo que no.

Sería lo mismo que contestar.

No, I don't think she's doing anything – No, no creo que ella esté haciendo algo.

Como siempre, deben repasar y aprender bien cada sección antes de continuar a la siguiente. A partir de esta lección, vamos a incluir una nueva sección en cada lección "***Word Definitions***". Esta nueva sección tendrá algunas palabras en inglés con sus definiciones en inglés.

Word Definitions

- ***Writer:*** *a person who writes in a particular way, books, stories, or articles as a job or occupation. Someone who has written something.*

- ***Famous:*** *known or recognized by many people. Having fame and widely known.*

- ***Usher:*** *a person who leads people to their seats in a theater, at a wedding, etc.*

- ***Groom:*** *a man who has just been married or is about to be married.*

- ***Bride:*** *a woman who has just been married or is about to be married.*

- ***To shoot:*** *kill or wound (a person or animal)*

with a bullet or arrow. Fire a bullet from a gun or discharge an arrow from a bow. Use a firearm with a specified degree of skill.

✒️ Exercises – Ejercicios

Exercise 2.1: Underline the word that does not belong (that is not in the same category as the others).

Example: told   expected   smoked   ask

1. tourist barber shop   museum   supermarket
2. turn   jail   expect learn
3. loud   noisy   noisily high
4. left   right   straight ahead   ground
5. band   professor   groom aunt

Exercise 2.2: Write the correct form of the verbs in parentheses. All of the sentences are in the simple past. Remember not to use the past after *did.*

Did you already _pay_ (pay) for your hotel room?

No, I didn't (1) _____ (say) I cannot make a

reservation. You (2) _____ (speak) too quickly.

You did not (3) _____ (understand) my question.

If you already (4) _____ (pay), you would lose

your money if you stayed somewhere else.

Margaret (5) _____ (look) everywhere for the

gold ring. But she (6) _____ (can) not find it. She

(7)_____ (get) down on her knees to look under

the couch. But it (8) _____ (be) not there. She

finally (9) _____ (sit) down on the floor,

discouraged. And then she (10) _____ (see) it on

top of the chair opposite her. She almost (11)

_____ (cry), she was so happy!

Exercise 2.3: Unscramble the sentence. Write the words in the correct order.
Example: at / turn / traffic light / the / don't / right
Don't turn right at the traffic light.
1. noisily / down / the hall / the guest / walked
2. the bridge / the groom / kissed / quickly
3. the class / quietly / boring / he / left
4. the rings / they / happily / for / paid / gold
5. the hall / artist's / the / across / is / studio

Exercise 2.4:
Make indirect questions. Add a phrase to make the sentence more polite.
Example: Why are you sad? _May I ask why you are sad?_
1. Where is the restroom?

_____

2. What is your name? _____

3. Where are you from?

_____

4. When does the movie start?

_____

5. Where is the museum?

_____

Lesson 3
The robbery – El robo

Conversation

Customer: Excuse me. Could you help me, please?

Clerk: Sure. What can I do for you?

Customer: Could I see the ring with all the little diamonds?

Clerk: The silver one?

Customer: No, the other one, the one with the diamonds in the shape of a flower.

Clerk: Ah. The gold one. Here it is.

Customer: Yes. Is it okay if I put it on?

Clerk: Well, um, okay, I guess so. The silver ring is also very popular.

Customer: It's kind of boring, though.

Clerk: It has less detail, but touch it. See how comfortable it is. All those details can hurt a lady's hand when the ring moves. The silver ring is very practical.

Customer: Yes, ... but she would like the gold one better.

Clerk: Okay. Would you like to set up payments or . . . . ?

Customer: I have a traveler's check.

Clerk: I'm sorry, Sir, but we don't accept traveler's checks.

Customer: Okay. Well, here, here's my credit card.

Clerk: Hmmm. It says payment is denied.

Customer: Do you mind if I use your phone?

Clerk: No problem.

Customer: I'd like to place a collect call. . . . Hi. Yes, I know you have an 800 number. I'm sorry I didn't bring it with me. I'm on vacation. I think my card is blocked. I'm at the jewelry store, and I'm trying to buy a ring. . . . Yes, that would be great. Thank you! Okay. Can you try it again?

Clerk: Sure. Oh, I'm sorry. Our system is down. Do you have cash?

Customer: No. I'm on vacation.

Clerk: How about I fill out a pen-and-paper charge slip?

Customer: Um, no. Let's just forget about it.

[Men with hankerchiefs over their mouths enter, waving guns around.] Put your hands up! Put everything in this bag. . . . Give me your wallet—oh, great. He has a gun. [The men run out of the store with the sound of gunfire.]

Clerk: Where are the police? Were you shot?

Customer: No, they fired the gun by accident. I'm fine.

Clerk: Thank you so much, Sir. Do you want to try to run your credit card through the system again?

Customer: No, thanks. I just want to know where to go to report the attempted robbery.

New words – Nuevas palabras
Boxing – boxeo
Champion – campeón
Foot – feet – pie / pies
Millionaire - millonario

Movie star – estrella de cine
Politician - político
Politics - política
Prime minister – primer ministro
Accident - accidente
Arm - brazo
Diamond - diamante
Ear – oreja / oído
Earring – arete / pendiente
Finger – dedo (de la mano)
Gold - oro
Ground – suelo / tierra
Gun - arma
Handkerchief – pañuelo
Jewel - joya
Jewelry – joyería
Karate - karate
Meal - comida
Mouth - boca
Neck - cuello
Necklace - collar
Nose - nariz
Note - nota
Ring - anillo
Thief – ladrón
Robbery - robo
Tooth – teeth – diente / dientes
Wallet - cartera
Age - edad
Call - llamada
Change - cambio
Clothes - ropa

Coin - moneda
Cow - vaca
Apartment - departamento
Driver's license – licencia de conducir
Foreigner – extranjero
Identification – identificación
Line - linea
Operator - operador
Paper – papel
Pen – lapicero / bolígrafo
Pepper - pimienta
Receiver – receptor / auricular
Sales - ventas
Salt - sal
Sheep - oveja
Traveler's check – cheque de viajero
Besides – además
Into – hacia adentro

Word Definitions
Suddenly: *very quickly, usually as a surprise.*
Collect call: *when the person who gets the call (not the person who is calling) pays for the call.*
Coin: *a piece of metal issued by the government to use as money.*
To dial: *establish or try to establish a telephone connection by operating the dial on a telephone.*
To ring: *give a clear resonant sound, as a bell when struck.*

Phrases and Expressions - Frases y expresiones
To answer the phone – contestar el teléfono

Forget it - olvídalo
Hold the line – espera en la línea
On the phone – al teléfono
To be robbed – ser robado
Man – hombre (expresión al hablar)
To be shot – ser baleado / recibir un tiro.

Grammar – Gramática

Vamos a aprender el uso de nuevos pronombres. Presten mucha atención a la forma en cómo se usan. Verdaderamente no existe una diferencia entre ellos, con excepción que la forma "body", que es un poco menos formal que la forma "one".

Pronouns in affirmative sentences – Pronombres en oraciones afirmativas.
Everybody – todo el mundo *(personas)*
Everyone – cada uno *(personas)*
Everything – todo *(cosas)*
Everywhere – en todo lugar *(lugar)*
Somebody – alguien *(personas)*
Someone - alguien *(personas)*
Something - algo *(cosas)*
Somewhere – en algún lugar *(lugares)*

There is *somebody* at the door – there is someone at the door – hay alguien en la puerta.

I would love to go *somewhere* this week – me encantaría ir a algún lugar esta semana.

Someone gave me a present – alguien me dio un regalo.

I am not goint to tell my secret to *anyone* – no le contaré mi secreto a nadie.

I gave you *everything* I had – te di todo lo que tenía.

Pronouns in interrogative sentences – pronombres en oraciones interrogativas

Anybody – alguien *(personas)*
Anyone – alguien *(personas)*
Anything – algo *(cosas)*
Anywhere – algún lugar *(lugares)*

Is (there) *anybody* home? – Is (there) anyone home? – ¿hay alguien en casa?

Did *anyone* come? - ¿vino alguien?

If you need *anything*, just tell me - si necesitas algo, solo dime

Pronouns in negative sentences – Pronombres en oraciones negativas

Nobody – *anybody – nadie *(personas)*
No one – anyone – nadie *(personas)*
Nothing – anything – nada *(cosa)*
Nowhere – anywhere – en ningún lugar *(lugares)*

I don't want to go *anywhere* with you – no quiero ir a ningún lado contigo.

I don't have *anything* to eat – no tengo nada de comer.

I can't find *anyone* – no puedo encontrar a nadie.

Es muy importante entender que cuando la oración esta en negativo, solo se podrán usar los que comienzan con "any".

Cuando usamos "*nobody, no one, nothing, nowhere*", la oración está en afirmativo, pero con un significado negativo. Veamos.

There is *nothing* I can do – no hay nada que yo pueda hacer.

There is *nowhere* you can go – no hay lugar donde puedas ir.

She has *nobody* to talk to – ella no tiene a nadie con quien hablar.

There was *no one* at the party – no había nadie en la fiesta.

Cuando una de estas palabras es usada como el sujeto de la oración, entonces es seguido por la conjugación del verbo para "he / she".

Everybody loves him – todo el mundo lo ama

Everything is ready – todo está listo

Everybody wants to go – todo el mundo quiere ir.

Everybody knows the truth – todo el mundo sabe la verdad.

Everything looks nice – todo luce bien.

Recuerden que "*somebody*" es para referirse a una sola persona. Si queremos referirnos a más de una persona, usamos "*some people*".

Somebody wants to see you – alguien quiere verte.

Some people want to see you – algunas personas quieren verte.

Nobody came to the church yesterday – nadie vino a la iglesia ayer.

Somebody left a message for you – alguien dejó un

mensaje para ti.

Podemos usar *"someone, something, somebody, somewhere"* en preguntas. Pero cuando lo usamos en preguntas, es porque estamos esperando que nos contesten con "Sí", es decir, que la respuesta sea positiva.

Are you going *somewhere?* - ¿vas a algún lado?
Yes, I am going home – Sí, voy a casa.
Are you looking for *something?* - ¿estás buscando algo?
Yes, I am looking for my watch – Si, estoy buscando mi reloj.
Can *somebody* help me, please? - ¿puede alguien ayudarme, por favor?
Yes, I can help you. – Si, puedo ayudarte.
Are you looking for *someone?* - ¿estás buscando a alguien?
Yes, I am looking for my sister – Si, estoy buscando a mi hermana.

Ahora, si hacen sus preguntas en formas negativas, es porque están 100% seguros de que la respuesta es "Sí", sin lugar a dudas. Veamos.
Aren't you going *somewhere?* - ¿no vas a algún lado?
Yes, I am going home – Si, voy a casa.
Aren't you looking for *someone?* - ¿no estás buscando a alguien?
Yes, I am looking for my sister – Si, estoy buscando a mi hermana.

Aren't you looking for *something*? - ¿no estás buscando algo?

Yes, I am looking for my watch – Si, estoy buscando mi reloj.

Tambien hay que tener mucho cuidado con este estilo, puesto que en muchos casos las usamos para cuestionar a la persona "aren't you going somewhere? Ya vete, no?"

Relative pronouns as a subject "Who / That" – Pronombres relativos como sujeto "Who / That".

Recordemos el significado de "who – quien" y "that – eso, esta". Los pronombres relativos siempre son seguidos por la conjugación del verbo en la tercera persona singular o plural. Podemos usar "who – that" para personas, pero cuando nos referimos a cosas solo podemos usar "that". No olviden que en este contexto, "that" lo traducimos como "que".

I lost the money – perdí el dinero.

I am the one *who* lost the money – soy quien perdió el dinero.

I am the one *that* lost the money – soy quien perdió el dinero.

These flowers are very expensive – estas flores son muy caras.

These are the ones *that* are very expensive – Esas son las que son muy caras.

I am the one *who* knows everything – soy el que sabe todo.

You are the man *who* is learning English – tú eres el hombre que (quien) está aprendiendo inglés.

Noten que casi siempre usamos "the one – el que / la que" cuando nos referimos a personas.

The one *who* is looking at you – el que te está mirando.

The one *that* is looking at you – el que te está mirando.

I want the expensive ice cream. I want the one *that* is expensive – quiero el helado barato. Quiero el que es barato.

Recuerden,

Cuando "who / that" se refieren al objeto de la oración, no es obligatorio usarlos. Podemos omitirlos. Veamos.

I have the contract. Peter signed it. – Tengo el contrato. Peter lo firmó.

I have the contract *(that)* Peter signed – tengo el contrato que Peter firmó.

This is the man. I hit him – este es el hombre. Yo lo golpeé.

This the man *(who[m] / that)* I hit – este es el hombre (a quien – que) yo golpeé.

Question words plus infinitive / Present progressive – Palabras interrogativas más el infinitivo / Presente progresivo.

We know *who to call* – sabemos a quién llamar.

We know *who we are calling* – sabemos a quién estamos llamando.

We know *what to do* – sabemos qué hacer.

We know *what we are doing* – sabemos lo que

estamos haciendo.

We know *when to leave* – sabemos cuándo partir.
We know *when we are leaving* – sabemos cuándo partiremos.

We know *where to go* – sabemos a dónde ir.
We know *where we are going* – sabemos a dónde vamos.

We know *how to get there* – sabemos cómo llegar.
We know *how we are getting there* – sabemos cómo llegaremos.

Como pueden ver, el uso es bastante sencillo, pueden usar tanto el infinito como el presente progresivo. Veamos algunos ejemplos en preguntas y respuestas.

Do you *know who(m) to call?* – ¿sabes a quien llamar?
Yes, I know *who(m) to call* – sí, sé a quién llamar.
No, I don't know *who(m) to call* – no, no sé a quién llamar.

Do you know *who you are calling?* – ¿sabes a quien estas llamando?
Yes, I know *who I am calling* – sí, sé a quién estoy llamando.
No, I don't know *who I am calling* – no, no sé a quién estoy llamando.

Do you know *what to do?* – ¿sabes qué hacer?

Yes, I know *what to do* – sí, sé qué hacer.
No, I don't know *what to do* – no, no sé qué hacer.

Do you know *what you are doing*? - ¿Sabes lo que estás haciendo?
Yes, I know *what I am doing* – sí, sé lo que estoy haciendo.
No, I don't know *what I am doing* – no, no sé lo que estoy haciendo.

Do you know *when to leave*? - ¿Sabes cuándo partir?
Yes, I know *when to leave* – si, se cuándo partir.
No, I don't know *when to leave* – no, no sé cuándo partir.

Do you know *when you are leaving*? - ¿sabes cuándo te marchas?
Yes, I know *when I am leaving* – sí, sé cuándo me marcho.
No, I don't know *when I am leaving* – No, no sé cuándo me marcho.

Do you know *where to go*? - ¿sabes a dónde ir?
Yes, I know *where to go* – si, sé a dónde ir.
No, I don't know *where to go* – no, no sé a dónde ir.

Do you know *where you are going*? - ¿sabes a dónde vas?
Yes, I know *where I am going* – sí, sé a dónde voy.
No, I don't know *where I am going* – no, no sé a dónde voy.

Do you know *how to get there?* - ¿sabes cómo llegar?

Yes, I know *how to get there* - sí, sé cómo llegar.

No, I don't know *how to get there* - no, no sé cómo llegar.

Do you know *how you are getting there?* - ¿sabes cómo llegaras?

Yes, I know *how I am getting there* - Si, sé cómo llegare.

No, I don't know *how I am getting there* - no, no sé cómo llegare.

Como pueden ver, las preguntas y respuestas siempre van con el "do" aun cuando estamos usando el presente progresivo, porque la primera parte de la oración está en presente simple. Y si se fijan bien, solo la primera parte está en forma de pregunta, la segunda no. Si quieren hacerlo en forma negativa, solo tienen que usar el negativo.

Do you know *what to do?* - ¿sabes qué hacer?

I don't know *what to do* - no sé qué hacer.

Do you know *what you are doing?* - ¿sabes lo que estás haciendo?

I don't know *what I am doing* - no sé lo que estoy haciendo.

Conjunctions - Conjunciones

Vamos a aprender a usar "**when - cuando**" y "**while - mientras**" como conjunciones.

Usamos "*while*" cuando dos cosas pasan al mismo tiempo.

My mother usually sings *while* she is cooking – mi mamá usualmente canta mientras está cocinando.

I sang *while* I played the piano – canté mientras tocaba el piano.

Si algo está sucediendo y entonces sucede algo más, usamos "*when*".

I talk. Everybody listens – hablo. Todos escuchan.

Everybody listens *when* I talk – todos escuchan cuando hablo.

The thief saw the police officer. She ran. – la ladrona vio al policía. Ella corrió.

The thief ran *when* she saw the police officer – la ladrona corrió cuando vio al policía.

When I talk, everybody listens – cuando hablo todos escuchan.

While I am cooking, I usually listen to the radio – mientras estoy cocinando, usualmente escucho la radio.

Pronouns and adjectives – Pronombres and adjetivos.

Continuemos aprendiendo otros pronombres y adjetivos.

Another – otro

Usamos **another** cuando hablamos del singular o queremos una cosa del montón. Es un adjetivo. Es "*an + other*" pero cuando los usamos juntos se convierten en una sola palabra. Expresa cantidad y significa "*uno más o adicional*".

I want *another* apple – quiero otra manzana.

Do you want **another** piece of fruit? - ¿quieres otra fruta?

Yes, I want **another** one. – sí, quiero otra.

No, I don't want any more – no, no quiero más.

También podemos usar "**another**" con "**one**" cuando en la frase o la oración está clara la alusión al texto anterior.

You ate a lot of apples. You can't eat **another one**. – comiste muchas manzanas. No puedes comer otra.

Do you want another apple? - ¿quieres otra manzana?

No, thanks – no gracias,

Yes, I want **another one** – sí, quiero otra.

También puede significar "**algo alterno o diferente**".

I am not happy with this perfume. Next time I am going to buy **another** brand – no estoy contento con este perfume. La próxima vez compraré otra marca.

Other – otro

Es un adjetivo y significa "diferente o el segundo de dos cosas". Podemos usarlo cuando hablamos del singular o plural.

I can't find my **other** key – no puedo encontrar mi otra llave.

Do you have any **other** questions? - ¿tienes alguna otra pregunta?

Yes, there are other questions to answer. – sí, hay otras preguntas para contestar.

No, I don't have any more questions. – no, no tengo más preguntas.

I want the **other** basket of apples – quiero la otra

canasta de manzanas.

También puede usarse con "*one – ones*" cuando el significado es claro por el contexto anterior.

I don't like this dog. I prefer *the other one* – no me gusta este perro. Prefiero el otro.

These shoes are nice, but *the other ones* look better – estos zapatos son lindos, pero los otros son mejores.

También podemos usar "*the other – the others*" como pronombres para referirnos a personas o cosas.

The others (the other people) are always ready – los demás siempre están listos.

Where are *the others*? - ¿Dónde están los demás?

The others are not here – los demás no están aquí.

I want juice, but *the others* prefer wine – quiero jugo, pero los otros (los demás) prefieren vino.

You have one, and I am going to have *the other* – tú tienes uno y yo voy a tomar el otro.

Each other – ambos
They love *each other* – se aman ambos / el uno al otro.

Regular verbs – Verbos regulares
To happen – *happened* – suceder / ocurrir / pasar
To remember – *remembered* - recordar
To weigh – *weighed* - pesar
To kill – *killed* - matar
To rob – *robbed* – robar / atracar
To sign – *signed* - firmar
To thank – *thanked* - agradecer

To try – *tried* – tratar / intentar
To borrow – *borrowed* – tomar prestado *(se toma prestado algo de alguien)*
To carry – *carried* – cargar / llevar
To dial – *dialed* - marcar
To exchange – *exchanged* – intercambiar

Irregular verbs – Verbos irregulares
To begin – *began* – empezar / comenzar
To hang up – *hung up* - colgar
To hear – *heard* - escuchar
To ring – *rang* – sonar
To lend – *lent* – prestar *(se presta algo a alguien)*
To break – *broke* - romper
To catch – *caught* – atrapar / agarrar
To choose – *chose* – elegir / escoger
To lie – *lay* – yacer / tenderse
To steal – *stole* - robar
To wake up – *woke up* - despertarse
To lose – *lost* - perder
To put – *put* - poner
To win – *won* - ganar

Adverbs - Adverbios
Even – aun / incluso
Someday – algún día
Ever – alguna vez / una vez
Inside - dentro
Outside - fuera
Suddenly – de repente
Again – de nuevo / otra vez

Adjectives – Adjetivos

*A few – un poco

Representa una idea positiva y seguida del plural.

I have *a few* books – tengo pocos libros.

They still have *a few* good products – ellos aún tienen unos pocos productos buenos.

Si usamos "*few*" solo sin el artículo "*a*", entonces denota una idea negativa, significando "*casi nada*".

I have *few* good friends – tengo pocos amigos *(denotando que no tiene muchos amigos y que le gustaría tener más)*.

Awful – terrible / horrible
Crazy – loco / descabellado
Exciting – emocionante / excitante
Funny – divertido / gracioso
Political - político
Asleep – dormido / adormecido
Collect – recolecta / colecta

The Champion

How can someone prepare to be a good politician—through sports, through fighting? Ask boxing champion Vitali Klitschko. His childhood dream was to be like Bruce Lee. And he did become a sports hero. He is very tall, he has long arms, and he has a strong chin. But he also has special training techniques that allow him to use a different strategy for each person he fights. He lost only two professional fights, and those losses were because of injuries—a cut above his eye and a shoulder injury;

no one knocked him down. Vitali is the one who is famous for knockouts.

In real life, he is a champion in more than fighting. He was the first professional boxing world champion with a PhD. Vitali's brother followed in his footsteps, becoming world boxing champion and earning a doctorate in sports science. The two brothers work together in other areas as well.

So what prepares a boxing champion to be successful in politics? Is it strategy? Vitali also plays chess. He says that "chess is similar to boxing [because] you need to develop a strategy, and you need to think two or three steps ahead [of] . . . your opponent." The difference between chess and boxing, he says, is that in chess "nobody is an expert, but everybody plays. In boxing everybody is an expert, but nobody fights." And in politics? Who are the experts in politics?

Vitali Klitschko became involved in the Ukrainian democratic opposition movement. While he served in parliament, he protested against the president, Yanukovych. In that fight, around 100 protesters lost their lives before a peace deal promised new elections. The champion of human rights is now the mayor of Kiev, in Ukraine. When two political groups **merged** in 2015, Klitschko became the party leader. He says that what Ukraine needs is for everyone to have a decent job, to bring home enough money to live comfortably. Ukraine needs to honor those who gave their lives in the revolution of 2014 in order to make Ukraine a modern European democratic country.

📝 Exercises – Ejercicios

Exercise 3.1: Write "another," "the other," or "each other."

Example: They're so funny! The girls are teaching _each other_ how to dance.

1.   Would you like _____ piece of cake? We have a lot of cake!
2.   Your parents are so nice. I can see they really

love _____.
3.   I don't want the blue pen. It doesn't work. I want _____ one.

4.   I'm sorry to bother you again. Could you give me_____ coin? The machine didn't start.

5.   I didn't buy the purple dress. I got _____ one.

Exercise 3.2: Max offends people with his direct questions. Rewrite the questions as indirect questions, to make them more polite.

Where is the restroom? _Do you know where the restroom is?_
1.   Why is the bank closed?

_____

2.   How can I rent a boat?

_____

3. When does the boat come back?

_____

4. Where are the other boats?

_____

5. Who is the manager?

_____

Exercise 3.3: Norman is a know-it-all. Write sentences with "I know."

Example 1: "Why did Marcus leave?" _I know why he left._

Example 2: "How do we get to the zoo?" _I know how to get there._

1. "Where is the park?"

_____

2. "When does the movie start?"

_____

3. "What should I do?"

_____

4. "Who is your dad calling?"

_____

5. "Where is your sister going?"

_____

Exercise 3.4: Write the best word.

anyone   anything   everyone   nobody
    nothing   something

Example: One the table? There's _nothing_ on the table.

1.   I couldn't find _____ to eat.

2.   _____ told me yesterday was your birthday.

3.   I need _____ to open the box with.

4.   I didn't see _____.

5.   I thought you were sick. _____ said you were sick.

Lesson 4
Going for a walk – Dar un paseo

Conversation 1

Mattie: Wow, you look terrible, Hannah!

Hannah: Thanks a lot!

Mattie: What's the matter?

Hannah: Oh, everything. Everything's the matter.

Mattie: Do you want to go for a walk? You might feel better.

Hannah: Okay. I've just had a terrible day.

Mattie: Tell me about it.

Hannah: Well, first, I don't like my haircut at all, so it took me forever to do my hair. So then I was late for work, and my boss gave me a speech about the importance of punctuality. My project was somehow erased from the computer system, and I lost two hours while the IT man worked to recover it. So then I had to stay late to finish. Then I missed the bus and had to walk home. The next bus didn't stop for me, but it splashed mud all over me. And now, I tried to wash my clothes, but the washing machine won't start. So now I have to handwash the laundry. I don't know how it could be worse.

Mattie: Um, I just felt something wet.

Hannah: Wet? Water? Great! Now, it's raining! And my clothes are on the clothesline.

Conversation 2

Julie:	*[Doorbell rings]* Hi, neighbor!
Luther:	Hi, Julie. Are you ready to go?
Julie:	Yep. Thanks. I see you washed your car. It looks great!
Luther:	Thanks. So what have you done today?
Julie:	Well, I just basically got ready to go out.
Luther:	Really? That's all you did? *[laughs]*
Julie:	Well, yeah. It's my day off, so I usually just work on my graduate class. But today was more relaxed. I ironed my clothes while the washing machine was running. I curled my hair while I washed the dishes. I thought of ideas for my homework while I mopped. And I did my makeup while the floor was drying.
Luther:	So you did the laundry, did your hair, did the dishes, did your homework, did your makeup, and washed the floors, but you didn't really do anything. You work hard, don't you?
Julie:	That's kind of you to say so. What did you do today?
Luther:	Well, you know I have a difficult case right now, so I mainly spent my time researching similar cases to find some inspiration.
Julie:	When do you get out of work?
Luther:	At three.
Julie:	Really? That's early.
Luther:	Yeah, that gave me time to get a haircut and a shave.
Julie:	That's nice. So hey, my mom asked me

what I was doing, and I said I was going out with the neighbor. And she said, "Going out? On a date?" And I laughed.

Luther: Haha.
Julie: So ...
Luther: [smiles]So ....?
Julie: Is this a date?

Conversation 3

Jake: Got everything?
Nate: Yep. Let's go.
Jake: All right. Now, you have the map, the compass, the water, and a first-aid kit, right?
Nate: First-aid kit? Where are we going?
Jake: Well, you never know. Better safe than sorry.
Nate: All right. I'll go get it. Just a second.
Jake: Let's go.
Nate: There aren't any snakes up there, are there?
Jake: No, I don't think so.
Nate: You don't think so? Have you ever seen any?
Jake: No, but I've never been on that trail before.
Nate: You've never gone there before?
Jake: No. But they say it's great.
Nate: I hope so. Did you bring any food?
Jake: No.
Nate: Neither did I.

Jake: If we're lucky, maybe we'll find some poison mushrooms.

Nate: Very funny.

Jake: So, how are you doing at work?

Nate: Great. My boss thinks I'm pretty good. He has me installing roofs.

Jake: You're quite the success, huh?

Nate: I'm doing okay. So are you sure this is the right way?

Jake: I think so.

Nate: That's comforting. There isn't a clear path. And I'm afraid one of these rocks might slip and I could faa-aa-aall *[falling]*.

Jake: Now, aren't you glad we brought the first-aid kit?

Nate: Yeah, I guess so. Let's just wrap up my ankle and go back down.

Jake: Go back down? We're just getting started.

Nate: Well, I'm done. I have to—oh, no! Now, I won't be able to get up on the roof tomorrow.

Jake: I guess not. I'm sorry about that.

Nate: Oh, it's okay, I guess. I have to call my boss though. He's not going to be happy about this. I've already missed three days of work this month. . . . *[calling boss]* Hey, Fred, I have some bad news. I think I've sprained my ankle. Yeah, *[laughs]* I'm okay on the roof, but an absolute failure at mountain climbing. The thing is, I don't think I could get up on the roof tomorrow. . . . No, I mean, I can still finish the job. I just need to let my ankle heal first. . . . *Yeah. Thanks. See you tomorrow.*

New words – Nuevas palabras

Ashtray - cenicero

Boss - jefe

Dish - plato

Failure - fracaso

Faucet – llave / grifo

Leg - pierna

Neighbor - vecino

Past - pasado

Present - presente

Success - éxito

Water - agua

Date – fecha / cita (cuando vamos a divertirnos con alguien con interes romantico)

Haircut – corte de pelo

Housework – tareas del hogar

Invitation – invitación

Laundry – lavandería

Mountain - montaña

Plate – plato (refiriéndose al recipiente)

Shave - afeitada

Swimming – natación

Umbrella – sombrilla / paraguas

Walk - caminata

Washing machine – lavadora

Appointment – cita (mayormente refiriéndose a negocios y no diversión)

Both – ambos

Quiche - Tarta de huevo (usualmente con carge o vegetales)

Word Definitions

Just: *now, a few minutes ago.*

To look: *to turn your eyes so you can see. To go and see.*

Neighbor: *a person who lives near you.*

To miss: *regret the absence or loss. Fail to be present at or for. Fail to hit or strike.*

Haircut: *an act or instance of cutting the hair. The style in which the hair is cut and worn, especially men's hair.*

To invite: *to ask someone to go somewhere.*

Phrases and Expressions - Frases y expresiones

To do (wash) the dishes – lavar los platos

To do your homework – hacer la tarea

To do the housework – hacer los deberes de la casa

To do the laundry – lavar la ropa

To get a haircut – recortarse el pelo

To get a shave - afeitarse

To go for a drive – dar un paseo en vehículo

To go for a meal – salir a comer

To go for a swim – salir a nadar

To go for a walk – salir a caminar

That's quite all right – está muy bien. Está bien, no hay inconvenientes.

That's very kind of you – es muy gentil (amable) de tu parte.

Grammar – Gramática

Hemos aprendido los tiempos gramaticales más importantes y primordiales. Estamos listos para

hablar del "*presente perfecto*".
Present perfect tense – Tiempo presente perfecto.
Ya somos expertos, de modo que no tienen que alarmarse. El presente perfecto funciona igual que en español. Se usa la conjugación de "*to have – haber*" en presente más el *pasado participio* del verbo. En inglés a diferencia del español, el pasado simple de los verbos regulares es el mismo que el pasado participio; en otras palabras es mucho más fácil en inglés. Solo debemos aprender el pasado participio de los verbos irregulares. Veamos un ejemplo.
I *kissed* the princess – besé a la princesa.
I *have kissed* the princess – he besado a la princesa.

Structure of the Present perfect – Estructura del presente perfecto.
Affirmative - afirmativo
I *have (I've) walked* – he caminado
You *have (you've) walked* – has caminado
He *has (he's) walked* – ha caminado
She *has (she's) walked* – ha caminado
We *have (we've) walked* – hemos caminado
You *have (you've) walked* – han caminado
They *have (they've) walked* – han caminado

Negative – negativo
I *haven't walked* – no he caminado
You *haven't walked* – no has caminado
He *hasn't walked* – no ha caminado
She *hasn't walked* – no ha caminado
We *haven't walked* – no hemos caminado

You *haven't walked* – no han caminado
They *haven't walked* – no han caminado

Questions – preguntas

Have I *walked?* - ¿he caminado?
Have you *walked?* - ¿has caminado?
Has he *walked?* - ¿ha caminado?
Has she *walked?* - ¿ha caminado?
Have we *walked?* - ¿hemos caminado?
Have you *walked?* - ¿han caminado?
Have they *walked?* - ¿han caminado?

Como pueden ver, no es nada complicado; de hecho es más fácil que en español y la estructura funciona igual que en el idioma español. Practiquemos un poco este tiempo con verbos regulares e irregulares en el pasado participio.

I've already ***been*** there – ya he estado ahí.
I ***haven't been*** there yet – aún no he estado ahí.
I've just ***been*** there – acabo de estar ahí.
I've never ***been*** there – nunca he estado ahí.
Have you ever ***been*** there? - ¿alguna vez has estado allí?
No, never – no, nunca.
Yes, a few times – si, algunas veces.

Have you ever ***studied*** English? - ¿alguna vez has estudiado inglés?
Yes, *I've* already ***studied*** English – sí, ya he estudiado inglés.
No, *I have* never ***studied*** English – no, nunca he

estudiado inglés.

I've just *studied* English – acabo de estudiar inglés.

Es bastante sencillo; solo necesitamos practicar. Recuerden algunas notas importantes sobre estas palabras que hemos estado usando, dándole un mejor sentido a la oración.

Yet – todavía / aun
Solo se usa en preguntas y respuestas negativas. Y usualmente viene al final de la oración.

Just – solo / reciente
Siempre viene entre en verbo auxiliar "have / has" y el verbo principal.

Already – ya
Se usa en cualquier lugar.

Ever / never – alguna vez / nunca.
Solo se usa en preguntas y respuestas negativas y viene después del verbo auxiliar.

Past participle – Pasado participio
Existen cinco tipos de pasados participios en inglés.
El pasado participio de los verbos regulares, que es el mismo que el pasado simple.
To walk – *walked* – *walked* - caminar
To kiss – *kissed* – *kissed* - besar
To ask – *asked* – *asked* – pedir / preguntar
To have – *had* – *had* - tener
To clean – *cleaned* – *cleaned* - limpiar
To describe – *described* – *described* - describir
To fix – *fixed* – *fixed* – arreglar / reparar
To iron – *ironed* – *ironed* - planchar
To look – *looked* – *looked* – mirar / observar

To turn – *turned* – *turned* – girar / voltear

To wash – *washed* – *washed* - lavar

To worry – *worried* – *worried* - preocuparse

To invite – *invited* – *invited* - invitar

To miss – *missed* – *missed* – extrañar / faltar / errar

To refuse – *refused* – *refused* - rehúsar

To shave – *shaved* – *shaved* – afeitar

En el pasado participio algunos verbos usan la misma forma del pasado simple.

To feel – *felt* – *felt* - sentir

To tell – *told* – *told* - decir

El pasado participio de algunos verbos que es el mismo que el infinitivo.

To come – *came* – *come* - venir

To hit – *hit* – *hit* - golpear

To run – *ran* – *run* - correr

To become – *became* – *become* - convertirse

El pasado participio de algunos verbos que termina en "En, N".

To give – *gave* – *given* - dar

To fly – *flew* – *flown* - volar

To go – *went* – *gone* - ir

To break – *broke* – *broken* - romper

To choose – *chose* – *chosen* - escoger

To do – *did* – *done* - hacer

To drive – *drove* – *driven* - conducir

To eat – *ate* – *eaten* - comer

To forget – *forgot* – *forgotten* - olvidar

To get – *got* – *gotten* - obtener

To know – *knew* – *known* - saber

To lie – *lay* – *lain* - recostarse

To see – *saw* – *seen* – mirar / ver
To show – *showed* – *shown* - mostrar
To speak – *spoke* – *spoken* - hablar
To steal – *stole* – *stolen* – robar / hurtar
To take – *took* – *taken* – tomar / llevar
To wear – *wore* – *worn* - usar
To write – *wrote* – *written* - escribir
To be – *was / were* – *been* – ser o estar

El participio de algunos verbos que tienen "i" en el presente "a" en el pasado "u" en el participio.
To begin – *began* – *begun* – iniciar / comenzar
To sing – *sang* – *sung* - cantar
To swim – *swam* – *swum* - nadar
To drink – *drank* – *drunk* - beber
To ring – *rang* – *rung* - sonar

Aprendamos muy bien esta lista y el patrón mencionado, puesto que todos los verbos forman parte de una de estas cuatro divisiones. Continuemos practicando un poco más.

Has she *spoken* with you? - ¿ha ella hablado contigo?

Yes, she *has* already *spoken* with me – sí, ella ya ha hablado conmigo.

No, she *hasn't spoken* to me yet – no, ella aún no ha hablado conmigo.

What *have* you *told* them? - ¿qué les has dicho?

I *haven't told* them anything yet – aún no les digo nada.

I've told them the truth – les dije la verdad.

What *have* you *done*? - ¿Qué has hecho?

I *haven't done* anything – no he hecho nada.

I *have done* what you asked – he hecho lo que me pediste.

Have you *been* to Paris? - ¿has ido a Paris?

Yes, *I've* already *been* to Paris – sí, ya he estado en Paris.

Yes, *I've* just *come* from Paris – sí, acabo de llegar de Paris.

No, I *haven't been* to Paris yet – no, aún no he ido a Paris.

I *have* never *been* to Paris - nunca he estado en Paris.

Recuerden,

Usamos el pasado simple cuando algo ya no volverá a pasar, es decir, se quedó en el pasado.

Usamos el presente perfecto cuando pudiera volver o no a pasar, pero existe la posibilidad. Ya hemos aprendido el presente perfecto. Practiquemos y hablemos.

Have to – tener que

Ya vimos el verbo "***to have – tener***". Solo vamos a repasar un concepto muy sencillo cuando usamos "have + infinitive". Cuando usamos el "have" con el infinitivo del verbo, lo traducimos como "tener que". Veamos algunos ejemplos.

I *have to study* English – tengo que estudiar inglés.

She *doesn't have to study* hard – ella no tiene que estudiar duro.

I *had to study* yesterday – tuve que estudiar ayer.

I *am going to have to study* tomorrow voy a tener que estudiar mañana.

I *used to have to study* hard – solia tener que estudiar duro.

I've had to study hard all my life – he tenido que estudiar duro toda mi vida.

Vean la estructura en todos los tiempos, y practiquen. Su nivel de inglés es asombroso. Si han asimilado el contenido correctamente hasta ahora, ustedes están hablando inglés casi fluido.

Adverbs – Adverbios
Actually – realmente / en realidad
Fortunately - afortunadamente
Perhaps – tal vez
Soon - pronto
Unfortunately - desafortunadamente

Adjectives – Adjetivos
Electric - eléctrico
Great - grandioso
Kind – amable - bondadoso
Serious - serio

Exercises – Ejercicios
Exercise 4.1: Write the verb in the present perfect (have/has + past participle).
Example: "I_'ve_ just _finished_ my homework (finish)." / "Great! Do you want to go see a movie?"

1. "_____ you _____ any lunch (have)?" / "No." / "Do you want to go out to eat?"

2. "Did you find your keys?" / "I _____n't _____ for them yet (look)."

3. "I_____ _____ my dress shoes (ruin)!" / "Oh, no. What are you going to wear for your speech?"

4. "My parents _____ _____ the house (sell)." / "Wonderful! Now they can move to Florida."

5. "Do you want to see the new science fiction movie?" / "No, I_____ already _____ it (see)."

6. "_____ you_____ _____ to Charleston (be)?" / "Yes, it's beautiful!"

7. "Do you want some quiche?" / "Yes, please. I_____ never _____ it before (try)."

8. "Do you like your new pants?" / "I _____n't _____ them yet (wear)."

9. "_____ you ever _____ on an international flight (fly)?" / "No, just national ones."

10.

11. "I _____ _____ the computer (fix). You can use it now." / "Thanks so much!"

Exercise 4.2: Underline the correct vocabulary word.

1. My hair is really long. I need a (**haircut / meal / homework**).
2. Wow! This place is really dirty. We need to do some (**swim, homework, housework**).
3. Oh, no! The test is tomorrow, and I didn't do my (**haircut / homework / housework**).
4. I need some exercise. Let's go for a (**shave / swim / meal**).
5. I need a change of **scenery**. Let's go for a (**haircut / meal / drive**).

Exercise 4.3: Underline the correct word.

1. Have you (**ever/yet**) been to New York?
2. I have (**ever/already**) eaten lunch. I'm not hungry.
3. I've (**never/yet**) seen the ocean. I want to go next year.
4. What have you done lately? I've (**never/just**) finished writing a book.
5. Have you done your homework (**just/yet**)? There's a lot to do!

Lesson 5
Getting sick - Enfermandose

Conversation 1

Josh: Hi, Gene, how are you?

Gene: I'm okay. I have a little bit of a headache with all the work planning this dinner.

Josh: I'm sorry, but I'm afraid I feel worse than you.

Gene: Really? What's the matter?

Josh: I think I have the flu.

Gene: Are you throwing up?

Josh: Yeah, and I woke up in the middle of the night with nausea, so I took some pills. And now I have diarrhea.

Gene: Maybe you ate something that bothered your stomach.

Josh: Yeah, that must be it.

Gene: Well, I guess you'd better get some rest. Do you have ginger ale?

Josh: No, why? Is that good for the flu?

Gene: It really helps an upset stomach. Do you have a convenience store nearby?

Josh: Yeah. Just down the street.

Gene: Okay. Get yourself some ginger ale and salty crackers. Or you could eat some chicken noodle soup. When you're feeling a little better, you can eat rice, bananas, or toast, too.

Josh: I have some bean soup. How about that?

Gene: Bad idea, Josh. Stick to the crackers for now if you don't want to feel worse.

Conversation 2

Paul: All right, Shane, are you done studying? Let me give you a little quiz. Let's see. Let's say I have a sore throat.

Shane: No other symptoms?

Paul: No.

Shane: Take a little tea with honey and lemon.

Paul: Okay. And for a stomachache?

Shane: Well, it depends on the cause: you might have a virus or you could have eaten something that you need to get out of your system.

Paul: All right. And if I have a runny nose, sore throat, and a backache?

Shane: Sounds like a cold. Take some cough medicine and get a lot of rest.

Paul: Yep. And what if I feel dreamy and depressed?

Shane: Dreamy and depressed? Sounds like a sickness of the heart. Are you in love?

Paul: No, unfortunately. Well, you might pass your test. But you should probably keep studying all night. Do you have any symptoms?

Shane: Yeah. A pain-in-the-neck roommate!

Paul: Glad to help!

New words – Nuevas palabras
Ashtray - cenicero
Boss - jefe
Dish - plato
Failure - fracaso
Faucet – llave / grifo
Leg - pierna
Neighbor - vecino
Past - pasado
Present -presente
Success - éxito
Water - agua
Date – fecha / cita (cuando vamos a divertirnos con alguien con interes romantico)
Haircut – corte de pelo
Housework – tareas del hogar
Invitation – invitación
Laundry – lavandería
Mountain - montaña
Plate – plato (refiriéndose al recipiente)
Shave - afeitada
Swimming – natación
Umbrella – sombrilla / paraguas
Walk - caminata
Washing machine – lavadora
Appointment – cita (mayormente refiriéndose a negocios y no diversión)
Both – ambos
Quiche - Tarta de huevo (usualmente con carge o vegetales)

Word Definitions

Tasty: Having good flavor; yummy, delicious

Prescription: orders from the doctor for behavior or medicine to take

To examine to look over in order to evaluate

Patient: person being examined or treated by a doctor

Disease: serious illness

Flu: a virus causing vomiting and possibly diarrhea

Fever: consistently high temperature

Love at first sight: a romantic inclination that began from the first meeting

Phrases and Expressions - Frases y expresiones

Bless you – salud / bendición

Love at first sight – amor a primera vista

To be a pain in the neck – ser un fastidio

To be in love – estar enamorado

Different from – diferente de

To get sick - enfermarse

To get well - mejorarse

To get a disease – contraer una enfermedad

To have a look at – dar una mirada (ojeada)

To have an operation - operarse

To take someone's temperature – tomar la temperatura de alguien

What's wrong with…? - ¿Cuál es el problema con…? ¿Qué pasa con…?

The cost of living – el costo de la vida

To know why – saber el por qué

To understand why – entender el por qué

Grammar – Gramática

Ya hemos visto el *"would like"*, que es una forma del condicional. Veamos el *"would"* como condicional en su forma completa. Como verán, ya saben usarlo, aun antes de explicárselo. Pero les daremos un repaso para mejor aprendizaje.

Would - condicional

Podemos usarlo con cualquier verbo; para la estructura usaremos el verbo "to go". Recuerden que el condicional demuestra una posibilidad, sugerencia o invitación y equivale a la terminación "ría" en español.

Affirmative – afirmativo

I would (I'd) go – yo iría
You would (you'd) go – tú irías
He would (he'd) go – él iría
She would (she'd) go – ella iría
We would (we'd) go – nosotros iríamos
You would (you'd) go – ustedes irían
They would (they'd) go – ellos / ellas irían

Negative – negativo

I wouldn't go – yo no iría
You wouldn't go – tú no irías
He wouldn't go – él no iría
She wouldn't go – ella no iría
We wouldn't go – nosotros no iríamos
You wouldn't go – ustedes no irían
They wouldn't go – ellos / ellas no irían

Questions – preguntas
Would I go? - ¿iría yo?
Would you go? - ¿irías tú?
Would he go? - ¿iría él?
Would she go? - ¿iría ella?
Would we go? - ¿iríamos nosotros?
Would you go? - ¿irían ustedes?
Would they go? - ¿irían ellos / ellas?

Would you go with me to the movies tonight? - ¿irías conmigo al cine esta noche?
Yes, I'd go with you. – Sí, iría contigo.
No, I wouldn't go with you – no, no iría contigo.

I would go with you, but I don't have time – iría contigo, pero no tengo tiempo.
I would study with you, but I don't have the book – estudiaría contigo, pero no tengo el libro.
I would buy the book, but I do not have money – compraría el libro, pero no tengo dinero.
Como pueden ver, ya sabían cómo usarlo; la estructura o patrón es el mismo que usamos anteriormente. Practiquen lo más que puedan y hablen en todo momento.

Comparing people and things with adjectives – Comparando personas y cosas con adjetivos.
Cuando queremos comparar personas o cosas, siempre tenemos que usar el comparativo. Existen tres grados del comparativo como veremos mas abajo.

Equity – Igualdad

En español usamos la combinación *"tan... como"* para el comparativo de igualdad; en inglés usaremos *"as... as"*. Veamos.

You are **as** intelligent **as** you look – eres tan inteligente como pareces.

She is **as** tall **as** her sister – ella es tan alta como su hermana.

He is **as** ugly **as** his brother – él es tan feo como su hermano.

Si queremos usar el comparativo de igualdad en negativo, tenemos que usar *"not as...as"*.

He is **not as** ugly **as** his brother – él no es tan feo como su hermano.

She **isn't as** tall **as** her sister – ella no es tan alta como su hermana.

You are **not as** intelligent **as** you look – no eres tan inteligente como pareces.

Como ven, es bastante sencillo; el concepto es prácticamente el mismo que en español.

Superiority – Superioridad

En español usamos la combinación *"más...que"*; en inglés vamos a usar la combinación *"more...than"* y *"er...than"*

Cuando el adjetivo tiene *más de una sílaba,*

entonces usamos "*more...than*".

She is *more* important *than* you – ella es más importante que tú.

She is *more* beautiful *than* her sister – ella es más hermosa que su hermana.

You are *more* intelligent *than* me – tú eres más inteligente que yo.
Cuando el adjetivo tiene *una sílaba, o termina en "y" o "ly"*, entonces usamos "*er...than*".

She is tall*er than* her sister – ella es más alta que su hermana.
He is smart*er than* his brother – él es más inteligente que su hermano.
They are fast*er than* us – ellos son más rápido que nosotros.

Cuando termina en "*y*" o "*ly*", cambiamos la "*y*" por una "*i*" y le agregamos "*er*".
We are happ*ier than* them – somos más felices que ellos.
I am angr*ier than* you – estoy más enojado que tú.
She is ugl*ier than* you – ella es más fea que tú.
They are bus*ier than* you – ellas estan más ocupadas que ustedes.
I am funn*ier than* you – soy más divertido que usted.

Si el adjetivo de una sílaba termina en una consonante, tenemos que duplicar la consonante final antes de agregarle "*er*".

The water today is hot*ter than* yesterday – el agua hoy está más caliente que ayer.

She is wett*er than* you – ella está más mojada que tú.

No olviden la parte más importante: cuando la palabra tenga *más de una sílaba* siempre usamos "*more...than*" cuando es de *una sola sílaba o termina en "y" o "ly"*, entonces usamos "*er...than*".

También podemos usar "more...than" con verbos.

I study more than you – estudio más que tú.

I used to go out more than you – acostumbraba a salir más que tú.

Usando "*more...than*" o "*er...than*" con adverbios.

I run fast*er than* you – corro más rápido que tú.

You are *more* careful *than* me – eres más cuidadoso que yo.

Inferiority – Inferioridad

En español usamos la combinación "menos...que"; en inglés usaremos "*less...than*". Es muy importante que comprendan el concepto de "*less...than*" solo se usa cuando hablamos de cosas que no podemos contar, como "information".

I have *less* information *than* you – tengo menos información que tú.

The apple cost *less than* I thought – la manzana costó menos de lo que pensé.

Como pueden ver, pueden usar una palabra en medio de "less...than" o no; depende de ustedes.

The apple cost *less (money)* *than* I thought – la manzana costó menos de lo que pensé.

Para cosas contables, entonces tenemos que usar "*fewer...than*".

I have *fewer* books *than* you – tengo menos libros que tú.

I have *fewer than* five products – tengo menos de cinco productos.

Usando "less...than" con verbos.

I run *less than* you – corro menos que tú

I eat *less* now *than* I used to eat – ahora como menos que lo que acostumbraba a comer.

Como siempre, tenemos algunos que son irregulares y que tenemos que aprender de memoria.

Good / well – better - bueno

Bad – worse - malo

Little – less - poco

I am *better than* you – soy mejor que usted

She is *worse than* me – ella es peor que yo

Superlative – Superlativo

Como el nombre lo dice, el superlativo es para indicar que alguien o algo es lo máximo. En español usamos "*el más, el menos*". En inglés usamos "the" seguido de la terminación "est" para los regulares. Veamos las reglas en inglés.

Palabra o sílaba que termina en "e": le agregamos "st" para el superlativo.

She is *the nicest* girl in town – ella es la chica más linda del pueblo.

She is *the fastest* runner in the marathon – ella es la corredora más rápida del maratón.

Palabras o sílabas con una sola vocal y una consonante al final: se le duplica la consonante final y se le agrega "est".

Nicauris is *the hottest* girl in town – Nicauris es la chica más caliente del pueblo.

He is *the tallest* guy in the class – él es el hombre más alto de la clase.

You are *the biggest* clown in the world – eres el payaso más grande del mundo.

Palabras con una sílaba, con más de una vocal o más de una consonante al final: solo se le agrega "est".

This is *the highest* mountain in the world – ésta es la montaña más alta del mundo.

Palabras de dos sílabas terminando en "y": cambiamos la "y" por una "i" y agregamos "est".

I am *the happiest* man in the world – soy el hombre más feliz del mundo.

You are *the ugliest* girl in town – eres la chica más fea del pueblo.

You are *the prettiest* girl in the class – eres la chica más linda de la clase.

Palabras de dos o más sílabas que no terminan en "y": usamos "the most".

We are *the most popular* people in town – somos las personas más populares de la ciudad.

Nicauris is *the most beautiful* girl in my town – Nicauris es la chica más hermosa de mi pueblo.

You are *the most important* person in my life – eres la persona más importante en mi vida.

Irregular superlatives – Superlativos irregulares
Good / well – better – the best
Bad – worse – the worst
Little – less – the least

You are *the best* student in the class – eres el mejor estudiante de la clase.

You are *the worst* driver – eres el peor conductor.

You arc *the least* important person in my life – eres la persona menos importante en mi vida.

Con esto hemos concluido la parte del comparativo y superlativo. Asegúrense de practicar los conceptos presentados y hagan los ejercicios; de esto depende el éxito de su aprendizaje.

Auxiliary verb "must" – Verbo auxiliar "must".
Ya hemos aprendido los diferentes usos del "have to"; ahora vamos a aprender el uso del "must", que tiene el mismo significado en español: "tener que – deber"; pero en inglés tiene diferencia en su uso. *Recuerden, NUNCA se usa "TO" después de "must".*

Expresando una obligación o un deber.
You *must* take your medicine – tienes que tomarte tu medicina.

You *must* wear your seatbelt while you're driving – debes usar tu cinturón de seguridad mientras conduces.

You *mustn't* speak on the phone while driving – no debes hablar por teléfono mientras conduces.

Enfatizando la necesidad de algo.
You *must* drive carefully – debes conducir con cuidado.

You **must not** smoke, it is not good for your health – no debes fumar, no es bueno para tu salud.

She **must** study her lessons to learn English well – ella debe estudiar sus lecciones para aprender bien inglés.

Cuando estás seguro de que algo es cierto, una deducción segura.

Lo usamos cuando no sabemos, pero estamos seguros basados en hechos o experiencias.

Tiffany **must** be home. I heard some voices – Tiffany debe estar en casa. Escuché unas voces.

They **must** be hungry, it is 3 p.m., and they haven't eaten yet – ellos deben estar hambrientos, son las 3 p.m. y aún no han comido.

Dando una fuerte recomendación.

You **must** taste the food here – debes probar la comida de aquí.

We **must** get together sometimes – debemos juntarnos alguna vez.

You **must** hear "Messin' Around" by Pitbull. It is fantastic. – debes escuchar "Messin' around" de Pitbull; es fantástica.

Expresando suposiciones lógicas positivas "must+have+past participle".

It **must have rained** yesterday – debió haber llovido ayer.

You **must have won** the lottery with the new car you just bought – debiste haberte ganado la loto con el nuevo carro que acabas de comprar.

Yeiris **must have eaten** all the food; there's nothing left – Yeiris debió haberse comido toda la comida, no queda nada.

Recuerden, en sentido general cuando usamos "**must**"; éste indica algún tipo de obligación impuesto por el hablante.

En caso de que tengan que hacer alguna pregunta, entonces deben usar "**have to**"; el "**must**" por lo general no se usa para preguntar.

Adjectives – Adjetivos
Dry - seco
Easy – fácil
Friendly – amigable / amistoso
Healthy - saludable
Narrow - estrecho
Relaxed - relajado
Safe - seguro
Smart – inteligente / astuto / listo
Sour – agrio / amargo
Strange – extraño
Sweet - dulce
Tasty - sabroso
Wide - ancho
Comfortable – cómodo / confortable
Dangerous – peligroso
Difficult – difícil
Cheap - barato
Better - mejor
Glad – contento / alegre
Uncomfortable - incómodo
Economical - económico
Whole – todo / entero / total
Prepositions – Preposiciones
Because of – por motivo de

I cannot eat *because of* you – no puedo comer por ti (por tu culpa).

In the middle of – en medio de
The glass is *in the middle of* the table – el vaso está en medio de la mesa.

Since - desde
Expresa cuando inició algo que aún no ha terminado.

I've had this car *since* 2002 – he tenido esta carro desde el 2002.

I have been here *since* 1998 – he estado aquí desde el 1998.

New regular verbs – Nuevos verbos regulares
To compare – compared - compared - comparar
To visit – visited – visited - visitar
To breathe – breathed – breathed - respirar
To examine – examined – examined - examinar
To jump – jumped – jumped – saltar / brincar
To last – lasted – lasted – durar / perdurar
To smell – smelled – smelled - oler
To sneeze – sneezed – sneezed - estornudar
To taste – tasted – tasted – probar / saborear

New irregular verbs – Nuevos verbos irregulares
To hurt – hurt – hurt – lastimar / doler
To lie down – lay down – lain down - recostarse
To take off – took off – taken off – despegar / quitarse
To cost – cost – cost - costar

To find out – found out – found out - descubrir

Getting a filling

Gary called his friend's dental office in the middle of the afternoon. The secretary told him the dentist couldn't see him for two weeks. But Gary told her he had to see the dentist right away. He just couldn't take it anymore—his toothache was killing him. The secretary double-booked his appointment and told him they would try to fit him in that afternoon but she couldn't promise anything.

The dentist's waiting room was full when Gary got there. After a while, he was the only one left. And still, he waited. Finally, with only fifteen minutes left until closing, the dentist called him back.

"Gary, nice to see you. What's the matter?" asked the dentist. "Oh, it looks like you have a pretty bad cavity. You need a filling. Would you like me to schedule an appointment to fill your cavity?"

Gary asked, "Can't you do it now? It hurts so bad—more than any other toothaches I've ever had before."

"There really isn't time today. It's closing time."

"Please, Bill. I'd do anything to get rid of this pain."

"Tell you what. This is very unconventional, but I have a couple things I need to do tonight. If you can help me with one of them, I can fill your tooth.

"Sure. Bill, anything."

So the dentist filled his tooth. He first numbed Gary's gum. Then he used a syringe to insert an anesthetic so that the drilling wouldn't hurt. And it didn't hurt. Gary felt better than ever. Of course, his mouth was still numb.

"If you don't want to get a new filling every couple years, you must brush your teeth three times a day and floss," the dentist told Gary.

"So what's the favor you need?" Gary asked the dentist. He had to repeat himself a couple times. With his mouth numb, he was hard to understand.

"Ah," the dentist chuckled. "Mary wants a giant monster for her daughter's birthday party. I have the costume in the car."

"Are you serious?" Gary asked.

"Yes," the doctor answered. "That is one of two things I had to do tonight."

"What's the other thing," asked Gary, "if you don't mind telling me?"

"I have to write an article about time management. It's due tomorrow."

"I guess I'll enjoy being a monster more than writing an article!" Gary said, grateful at least to be feeling better.

Exercises – Ejercicios

Exercise 5.1: These sentences are missing something. Add *must (have)* or *have to* where appropriate.

1. It's 5:45. You leave now if you want to catch the bus.

2. I can't say no. My country needs me. I go.

3. Dan didn't come to work today. He be sick.

4. But, Mom, just look at all that snow! Do I **shovel** the sidewalk?

5. Ingrid looks pretty happy. She finished her project.

Exercise 5.2: Say the same thing in other words.
Example: I love you more than I love chocolate. (as much as) I don't love chocolate as much as I love you.
1. John is taller than me. (short)
2. Chocolate bars cost less than chocolate chips. (more)
3. No one in the class is as smart as my boyfriend. (smart—superlative)
4. Our house is the least attractive house on the block. (ugly—superlative)
5. It's wetter inside than outside! (dry)

Exercise 5.3: Find the rest of the sentence. Write the letter.
1. _____ They would give you a discount,

2. _____ I would eat my vegetables,

3. _____ My dog would go to school,

4. _____ We would help you with your work,

5. _____ I would give you my ice cream,

6. _____ Mr. Smith would explain it to us,

a. but they won't let him in.
b. but he was detained in traffic.
c. but you have to take your ID card.

d.   but I need it for my sore throat.
e.   but they don't taste good.
f.   but we're really busy.

Lesson 6
Five star hotel – Hotel cinco estrella

Conversation 1

Customer: Good evening. I booked a room a couple weeks ago on the Internet.

Desk Clerk: Good evening. Can I have your name, please?

Customer: Here. It's on my card.

Desk Clerk: Did you use this card to book the room?

Customer: Yes.

Desk Clerk: Would you like me to charge the room on this card?

Customer: Yes.

Desk Clerk: Okay. You're all set. Room number 22C. Would you like me to show you to your room?

Customer: [30 minutes later] Hi. It's me again. I, well, it's the room. I asked for nonsmoking, but the room smells like smoke, and it's really bothering me. I just can't stand cigarette smoke.

Desk Clerk: Neither can I. We'll see if we can fix that for you. Which room were you in? . . . We'll have it ready in 10 minutes. I'll call your room when it's ready.

Customer: [Ring] Your new room is ready for you now. Just come by the front desk for the key.

Desk Clerk: Here's your key. Sorry about the inconvenience. Will there be anything else?

Customer: Well, actually, is there anywhere I can buy a toothbrush? I can't believe I forgot my toothbrush.

Desk Clerk: It happens to everyone. Actually, I have a complimentary toothbrush I can give you. If you need any more towels or pillows or anything, just let me know. And you can call on the phone. You don't need to come to the desk.

Customer: No, five pillows is enough, thank you!

Conversation 2

Chad: Have you decided what to get Mom yet?

Sheryl: What to get Mom?

Chad: Yeah, you know, for Mother's Day.

Sheryl: Oh, no! I forgot. What are you getting her?

Chad: Well, you know, I've always sent her flowers. But I thought maybe the three of us could all go in together and buy Mom and Dad a night at the hotel by the lake.

Sheryl: Oh, that's a good idea. How much would it be?

Chad: Well, it'd cost us about $40 each.

Sheryl: That's not bad. Does it include a meal?

Chad: It includes continental breakfast, which is pretty nice there.

Sheryl: Yeah. What would it cost to include dinner, too?

Chad: I don't know. It'd depend on what she

ordered.

Sheryl: Yeah, I guess so.

Chad: Actually, they have a snack room, and she can get a snack anytime.

Sheryl: Sounds good. Have you talked to Gina?

Chad: Yeah. She said she likes the idea.

Sheryl: Okay. Do you want me to reserve the room?

Chad: No, I'll do it. I'll use the points on my card to get the special price.

Sheryl: Oh, great. So I'll send you a check?

Chad: That works. Thanks, Sheryl. Oh, and Sheryl?

Sheryl: Yes?

Chad: Happy Mother's Day!

Sheryl: Thanks, Chad.

New words – Nuevas palabras
Blanket – frazada / cobija
Hair dryer – secador de pelo
Pillow - almohada
Pillowcase – funda (tapa) de almohada
Receipt – recibo
Service - servicio
Sheet – sábana
Star - estrella
Towel - toalla
Ball – pelota / bola
Doorbell – timbre de puerta
Envelope – sobre
Fool - tonto
Hole - hoyo

Race - carrera
Song – canción
Stamp – sello / estampilla
Telegram - telegrama
Brush - cepillo
Comb - peine
Father's day – día del padre
Mother's day – día de la madre
Electric razor – rasurador eléctrico
Pajamas - piyama
Pocket - bolsillo
Sea – mar
Stone – roca / piedra
Suggestion - sugerencia
Tennis racket – raqueta de tenis
Weight - peso
None - ninguno
During - durante
Except - excepto

Word Definitions
Tired of: when you don't like something or someone anymore.

Foot: one meter (3.28 feet)

Jump up and down: when you jump in the air and come down again.

Filthy: something very dirty.

Fool: a person who is not smart (not a good word)

To promise: to pledge that you will or will not do something. To give your word and commit to it.

Phrases and Expressions - Frases y expresiones
As soon as possible – lo antes posible

Not ... at all – no ... del todo

I am not happy at all – no estoy del todo contento /
no estoy para nada contento.

To do your best – hacer lo mejor, dar tu mejor
esfuerzo

To have something ready – tener algo listo

If you don't mind – si no te importa

What a fool! – que tonto

On business – de negocio

Full of – lleno de

To put on weight – subir de peso

To lose weight – perder peso

Up and down – arriba y abajo *(ir de una lugar a
otro, una y otra vez)*

To look like – parecerse / ser similar

How are things? - ¿Cómo están las cosas?

What's new? - ¿Qué hay de nuevo?

Grammar – Gramática

Como hemos visto en las lecciones anteriores
existen muchas formas de hablar sobre el futuro, al
igual que en español. Vamos a aprender el auxiliar
"will" y sus diferentes usos.

The future with "Will" – El futuro con "Will"

Affirmative - Afirmativo

I will – I'll

You will - you'll

He will - he'll

She will - she'll

We will - we'll

You will - you'll

They will - they'll

Negative – Negativo

I will not – I won't -

You will not - you won't -

He will not – he won't -

She will not – she won't -

We will not – we won't -

You will not - you won't -

They will not – they won't -

Questions - Preguntas

Will I? -

Will you? -

Will he? -

Will she? -

Will we? -

Will you? -

Will they? –

Como habrán podido ver, la forma contracta del afirmativo solo tiene que substituir la "wi" de *will* por un apostrofe en todos los pronombres. Para el negativo, la forma contracta es irregular: "***won't***". No lo olviden. *"will" siempre irá acompañado de otro verbo en su forma infinitiva sin el "to"*. Vamos a ver los diferentes usos del "***will***" ahora.

Cuando hacemos predicciones sobre el futuro. Creemos o pensamos algo sobre el futuro.

You ***will enjoy*** her company, she is very funny. – disfrutarás de su compañía; ella es muy divertida.

I think it ***will rain*** tomorrow – creo que lloverá mañana.

I think I *will win* the gold medal – creo que ganaré la medalla de oro.

Cuando decidimos hacer algo inmediato. Decisiones rápidas.

I'll pick you up now – te recogeré ahora

We'll call a taxi for you – llamaremos un taxi para ti.

I think *I will go* right now – creo que me iré ahora mismo *(acabo de tomar esa desición)*.

Cuando hacemos una promesa, amenaza, invitación, orden, solicitud u ofrecimiento.

If you say something, you *will regret* it – si dices algo, lo lamentarás.

I *will kill* you if you do something like that – te mataré si haces algo así

Don't worry. I *won't tell* anyone – no te preocupes. No se lo diré a nadie.

I *will do* my best to help you – haré todo lo posible para ayudarte.

I *will have* the documents ready for tonight – tendré los documentos listos para esta noche.

Will you help me? - ¿me ayudaras?

Will you have some cake? - ¿aceptarás un poco de bizcocho?

Cuando son acciones repetitivas o hábitos.

Yeiris *will fall asleep* as soon she starts reading – Yeiris se quedará dormida desde que comience a leer. *(ella siempre lo hace)*

My car *won't go* faster than this – mi carro no irá más rápido de ahí *(siempre es así, es lo máximo que corre)*

Con algunas acciones y eventos pasando en el presente.

Will you have another glass of wine? - ¿quieres otro vaso de vino?

The car won't start – el carro no enciende.

The baby won't stop crying – el bebe no para de llorar.

Cuando alguien se rehúsa a hacer algo usamos "won't".

Your brother *won't listen* to anything I say – tu hermano no escuchará nada de lo que le diga.

I told her to clean the room, but I know she *won't do* it. – le dije que limpiara la habitación, pero sé que no lo hará.

Polite commands – Órdenes o mandatos de cortesía.

Si queremos que alguien haga o no haga algo, pero no conocemos a la persona bien, preguntamos.

Will you open the door, please? - ¿abrirás la puerta, por favor?

Would you open the door, please? - ¿abrirías la puerta, por favor?

Can you open the door, please? - ¿puedes abrir la puerta, por favor?

Could you open the door, please? - ¿podrías abrir la puerta, por favor?

También usamos esta forma para cuando conocemos la persona bien; esto demuestra cortesía al hablar.

Cuando conocemos la persona bien, decimos también.

I want you to open the door – quiero que abras la puerta.

I don't want you to open the door – no quiero que abras la puerta.

I'd like you to open the door – me gustaría que abras la puerta.

I'd like you not to open the door – me gustaría que no abras la puerta.

Don't open the door – no abras la puerta.

Do not open the door – no abras la puerta.

Volunteering – Ofreciéndose como voluntario.

Cuando quieres saber si alguien quiere que hagas algo, pero no conoces bien a la persona, preguntas.

Do you want me to open the door? - ¿quiere usted que abra la puerta?

Do you want me not to open the door? - ¿quiere usted que no abra la puerta?

Would you like me to open the door? - ¿le gustaría que abra la puerta?

Would you like me not to open the door? - ¿le gustaría que no abra la puerta?

Si conoces bien a la persona, entonces puedes decir.

I'll open the door – abriré la puerta.

Let me open the door – déjame abrir la puerta.

Allow me to open the door – permíteme abrir la puerta.

Presten mucha atención a la estructura y forma tanto del afirmativo como del negativo.

The auxiliary verb "Should" – El verbo auxiliar "Should".

Usamos el verbo auxiliary "should" para hacer sugerencias. Es bastante fácil usarlo. Recuerden, después de "should" NUNCA usen "to" con los verbos. Siempre va acompañado de un verbo.

Affirmative – Afirmativo
I should
You should
He should
She should
We should
You should
They should

Questions – Preguntas
Should I?
Should you?
Should he?
Should she?
Should we?
Should you?
Should they?

Negative – Negativo
I should not – shouldn't
You should not – shouldn't
He should not – shouldn't
She should not – shouldn't

We should not – shouldn't
You should not – shouldn't
They should not – shouldn't

Dando consejos, recomendaciones o sugerencias.
You should go to the movies tonight – deberían ir al cine esta noche.
You should see a doctor about that problem – deberías ver un doctor acerca de ese problema.
You should comb your hair – deberías peinarte el cabello.

Expresando una situación que mayormente estaría pasando en el presente.
I am going to call Tiffany. She *should be* at home now – voy a llamar a Tiffany. Ella debería estar en casa ahora.
You *should have* the money. I sent it yesterday. – deberías tener el dinero. Lo envié ayer.

Expresando una situación que mayormente pasara en el futuro, una predicción.
She *should be* fine tomorrow – ella debería estar bien mañana.
France *should win* the cup, because their team is better. – Francia debería ganar la copa, porque su equipo es mejor.

Expresando una obligación más cortés y suave que con el "must".
You *should pay* more attention to my instructions – deberías prestar más atención a mis instrucciones.
You *should never lie* to your parents – nunca

deberías mentirles a tus padres.

You *should be* here in 10 minutes – deberían estar aquí en 10 minutos.

Expresando cuando no se está cumpliendo con una obligación.

*En este caso usamos "**should+be+ing**".*

They *should be studying* for the exam – ellos deberían estar estudiando para el examen *(pero no lo están)*

You *should be taking* your pills – deberías estar tomándote tus pastillas *(pero no lo estás haciendo)*

She *should be looking after* the children – ella debería estar cuidando los niños *(pero no lo está haciendo)*

Expresando algo esperado en el pasado, pero que no pasó.

En esta caso usamos "***should+have+past participle***".

I *should have been* more understanding, but I wasn't. – debería haber sido más comprensible, pero no lo fui.

You *should have seen* her play the piano, but you didn't. – debiste haberla visto tocar el piano, pero no lo hiciste.

They *should have been* here, but they weren't. – ellos debieron haber estado aquí, pero no lo estuvieron.

Cuando estamos aconsejando a alguien que no haga algo, porque no es debido o es malo, usamos "shouldn't".

You *shouldn't talk* to your parents like that – no

deberías hablarle a tus padres de ese modo.

You *shouldn't be* here now – no deberías estar aquí ahora *(es peligroso o indebido)*

He *shouldn't smoke* – él no debería fumar (es perjudicial para su salud).

The verb "to get" – El Verbo "to get".

Hemos visto en el transcurso de las lecciones pasadas como se usa el verbo "to get" para formar otros verbos y expresiones. Este es un verbo que tenemos que prestarle mucha atención, debido a que se usa mucho en inglés y puede ayudarnos a formar cualquier oración.

To look for and find – buscar y encontrar.

I am going *to get a job* – voy a conseguir un trabajo.

To look and buy – buscar y comprar.

I am going *to get a book* – voy a comprar un libro.

To receive something – recibir algo.

I *got an email* from Nicauris – recibí un email de Nicauris.

To catch someone – atrapar a alguien.

I am going to get you – voy a atraparte.

Existen muchísimas cosas que podemos hacer y construir con el verbo "to get"; ya iremos adquiriendo esos conocimientos con la práctica.

Adjectives "no / any" and Pronouns "None / Any" – Adjetivos "no / any" y Pronombres "none / any".

Vamos a ver como usamos estos dos adjetivos y pronombres. Es realmente sencillo. Presten mucha atención.

Estas cuatro oraciones significan lo mismo.

There is *no* cold water – no hay agua fría.

There is *none* – no hay nada.

There isn't *any* cold water – no hay nada de agua fría

There isn't *any* – no hay nada.

Estas cuatro oraciones significan lo mismo.

There are *no* napkins – no hay servilletas

There are *none* – No hay ninguna.

There aren't *any* napkins– no hay ninguna servilleta.

There aren't *any* – no hay ninguna.

Como pueden ver, el "no" siempre va a modificar una oración en afirmativo, dándole el sentido de la negación.

Siempre usaremos "any" en oraciones negativas.

Conjunctions – Conjunciones

Veamos como usamos las conjunciones "*So / too / neither / not … either".* Ya hemos visto el uso en lecciones pasadas. Vamos a dedicarles una corta sección con los diferentes tiempos y usos.

Affirmative – Afirmativo

I am sad – estoy triste

So am I – yo también

I am, too – yo también

I am working – estoy trabajando

So am I – yo también

I am, too – yo también

I *am going to sleep – voy a dormir*

So am I – yo también

I am, too – yo también

I was glad – estaba contento
So was I – yo también
I was, too – yo también
I like to cook – me gusta cocinar
So do I – a mí también
I do, too – a mí también
I went to law school – fui a la escuela de leyes.
So did I – yo también
I did, too – yo también
I have been to Paris – he ido a Paris.
So have I – yo también
I have, too – yo también
I can dance – puedo bailar
So can I – yo también
I can, too – yo también
I could speak when I was two – podía hablar
cuando tenía dos años
So could I – yo también
I could, too – yo también
I'll leave now – me iré ahora
So will I – yo también
I will, too – yo también
She would love to sing – a ella le encantaría cantar
So would he – a él también
He would, too – a él también
I should leave now – debería irme ahora
So should I – yo también
I should, too – yo también
I must work soon – debo trabajar pronto
So must I – yo también
I must, too – yo también
Recuerden que pueden usar cualquier pronombre

personal con esta estructura. Es muy usada, de modo que les recomiendo que la estudien muy bien y la practiquen.

Negative – Negativo

I am not sad – no estoy triste
Neither am I – ni yo tampoco
I am not either – ni yo tampoco
I am not working – no estoy trabajando
Neither am I – ni yo tampoco
I am not either – ni yo tampoco
I *am not going to sleep – no voy a dormir*
Neither am I – ni yo tampoco
I am not either – ni yo tampoco
I wasn't glad – no estaba contento
Neither was I – ni yo tampoco
I wasn't either – ni yo tampoco
I don't like to cook – no me gusta cocinar
Neither do I – ni a mí tampoco
I don't either – ni a mí tampoco
I didn't go to law school – no fui a la escuela de leyes.
Neither did I – ni yo tampoco
I didn't either – ni yo tampoco
I haven't been to Paris – no he ido a Paris.
Neither have I – ni yo tampoco
I haven't either – ni yo tampoco
I can't dance – no puedo bailar
Neither can I – ni yo tampoco
I can't either – ni yo tampoco
I couldn't speak when I was two – no podía hablar cuando tenía dos años

126

Neither could I – ni yo tampoco
I couldn't either – ni yo tampoco
I won't leave now – no me iré ahora
Neither will I – ni yo tampoco
I won't either – ni yo tampoco
*She wouldn't love to sing – a ella no le encantaría
cantar*
Neither would he – ni a él tampoco
He wouldn't either – ni a él tampoco
I shouldn't leave now – no debería irme ahora
Neither should I – ni yo tampoco
I shouldn't either – ni yo tampoco
I mustn't work soon – no debo trabajar pronto
Neither must I – ni yo tampoco
I mustn't either – ni yo tampoco
Recuerden que cuando usan "neither", la oración
esta en afirmativo; con el uso del "neither", damos en
sentido de la negación.

Adjectives – Adjetivos
Blanket – frazada / cobija
Hair dryer – secador de pelo
Pillow - almohada
Pillowcase – funda (tapa) de almohada
Receipt – recibo
Service - servicio
Sheet – sábana
Star - estrella
Towel - toalla
Ball – pelota / bola
Doorbell – timbre de puerta
Envelope – sobre

Fool - tonto
Hole - hoyo
Race - carrera
Song – canción
Stamp – sello / estampilla
Telegram - telegrama
Brush - cepillo
Comb - peine
Father's day – día del padre
Mother's day – día de la madre
Electric razor – rasurador eléctrico
Pajamas - piyama
Pocket - bolsillo
Sea – mar
Stone – roca / piedra
Suggestion - sugerencia
Tennis racket –   raqueta de tenis
Weight - peso
None - ninguno
During - durante
Except – excepto

Adverbs – Adverbios
In a minute – en un minute / muy pronto
Right now – ahora mismo /inmediatamente
Later – más tarde / luego

New regular verbs – Nuevos verbos regulares
To apologize – apologized – apologized – ofrecer disculpas, disculparse
To change – changed – changed - cambiar
To complain – complained – complained - quejarse

To close – closed – closed - cerrar

To cry – cried – cried - llorar

To promise – promised – promised - prometer

To turn up – turned up – turned up – subir el volumen

To turn down – turned down – turned down – bajar el volumen

To brush – brushed – brushed - cepillar

To comb – combed – combed - peinarse

To shout – shouted – shouted – gritar / vocear / vociferar

New irregular verbs – Nuevos verbos irregulares

To keep – kept – kept – mantener / guardar

To throw – threw – thrown – arrojar / lanzar

To ride – rode – ridden – montar (bicicleta, caballo, etc.)

Celebrating Mother's and Father's day

For the mother of young children, Mother's Day may be one of the most ironic celebrations of the year. The media help everyone in the US remember to prepare for the second Sunday of May. The most difficult part of Mother's Day, however, is that there is no correct way to celebrate the day. Every child and husband wants Mom to feel unique and special.

Children don't have much money or experience to help them with getting an exciting gift. So Mom has to pretend she doesn't know what her children are doing as she provides the materials and cleans up afterwards. Often Dad can help, buying a cake or taking the family out to dinner. Without Dad's help, some children make their own inventions to honor Mother. They might make their own cards with special drawings, stickers, or glitter. They might take her breakfast in bed: burnt toast, runny eggs, or cereal with orange juice. Older children will make her a cake, but then sometimes the mother has to clean up the kitchen afterward. If the family doesn't have the surprise ready in time, Mother may be isolated from the others while they finish.

Husbands often buy their wives and mothers cards, jewelry, clothes, or flowers. Actually, flowers have been a tradition on Mother's Day for over a hundred years, particularly carnations. Churches and stores sometimes give out carnations on Mother's Day: red or pink are for women whose mother is still living, and white for women whose mother has died.

Father's Day, celebrated in the US on the third Sunday of June, has not become as popular as Mother's Day. It's usually up to Mom to make Daddy's day special. She might decorate the house with paper ties or give him a decorated set of his favorite treats. But it's harder to make something that Dad will like. Some dads enjoy cards or ties on this day. But many would prefer more expensive gifts: tools, cars, or fishing poles. So most fathers probably only get a special meal. And some dads just get a friendly phone call or best wishes.

Exercises – Ejercicios

Exercise 6.1: You're out of everything! Write *there isn't any more* or *there aren't any more*. If it's countable, use the plural (*aren't*).

Example: Can I have some bread?   _There   isn't
any more._

   1.   I'd like some orange juice.

_____

   2.   These French fries are cold. You should give

me another box.   _____

   3.   Will you bring some of your brownies?

_____

   4.   Can I borrow some tape?

_____

   5.   Could you pass me the rolls?

_____

Exercise 6.2:   **You will not be outdone! Agree
with everything they say. (You only need to use one
method—*so* OR *too*.)**

Example 1:   It was terrible. I cried and cried.
  So did I. / I did, too.
Example 2:   I didn't see anyone I knew.
  Neither did I. / I didn't either.

   1.   I can play the glockenspiel.

_____

2. I should leave now.

_____

3. I was at the concert last night.

_____

4. I didn't like the spaghetti.

_____

5. I'll go the party after work.

_____

Exercise 6.3: **Underline the best request for the situation.**

1. Mother to little boy: I want you to do your homework. / Could you do your homework, please?

2. Man to boss: Can you send me that file again, please? / Send me the file again.

3. Child to aunt: I'd like you to give me some juice. / Can I have some juice?

4. Clerk to customer: Could you sign here, please? / I want you to sign here.

5. Woman to best friend: Would you not open the door, please? / Don't open the door.

Conversational Level Two – Nivel de Conversación Dos

Singing like a bird

Mary sings in the shower. It's one of those times when she feels uninhibited and completely happy. She feels like a fairy princess. The birds sing with her, providing harmony and orchestra.

"O mío babbino caro," she began one day. The birds sang along. Little butterflies hovered by the exhaust fan. One or two got too close.

Suddenly a load roar silenced everything else. Mary finished her shower. When she opened the door and saw her husband, she complained, "Ralph, you scared all the birds away."

"No, I didn't."

"Yes, you did. Listen. Do you hear birds singing?"

"Well, you're not in the shower anymore. They like the sound of the water." Ralph saw his wife was not convinced. "I suppose you're going to blame me for the butterfly wing in the exhaust fan, too, right?" he asked.

"Oh, poor little thing. He must have gotten too close."

"Really, Mary, you should make a CD—you and your birds and butterflies," Ralph said, laughing.

"Thanks." Mary ignored the sarcasm. "I've

practiced for a long time."

"Well, so have I," argued Ralph. "In fact, that's where I learned to sing—in the shower. And I think the birds could appreciate my superior talent."

"Superior to what?"

"You won't hear a better shower singer in the neighborhood," Ralph boasted.

"Whatever you say!"

"I sing as well as you," Ralph insisted.

"You don't sing, Ralph. You shout."

"Oh, so you don't want me to take a shower?"

"No, no. Please do. Be my guest. If it's not your singing, it'll be your smell that will keep the birds away."

For a couple minutes, all Mary heard was the calming sound of the water. Then it started. He was singing in the rain. He sang the same line over and over again—not two times, but eight times! Then it was a sad romantic song. He sang about war, faithful dogs, and his favorite foods.

Now, the bathroom had no window, but the exhaust fan was installed on a wall of the house that was near the street. And since it was a hot day, the windows were open anyway. And the neighbors could hear him. Nobody said anything, but they all rolled their eyes when they heard him and turned on their radio or TV to drown out the noise.

But Mary was not as lucky as her neighbors. She could not drown out the noise, no matter how loud she turned up the radio. Ten minutes went by, twenty. He was still happily shouting in the shower. Finally, Mary couldn't take it anymore, so she started to wash the dishes.

"Augh!... Hey, turn off the sink!"

"I'm sorry, Honey," she said, but you've been in there forever. If I wait any longer, there won't be any water left to wash the dishes. Besides, you don't want to damage your voice. Where would we be without our family's most valuable resource?"

"Very funny," he said. "Okay. I'll be out in a minute. I'll come and give you a private concert so you can hear me better."

Phrases and Expressions

Singing like a bird – cantando como una ave *(cuando canta muy bien)*

When she feels uninhibited - cuando ella se siente libre *(uninhibited se refiere a cuando puedes expresarte sin ningún inconveniente)*

Like a fairy princess – como una princesa de hada.

A load roar silenced – un fuerte rugido silenció

You scared all the birds away – asustaste todos los pájaros *(scare away es ahuyentar del susto)*

Be my guest – adelante *(es una expresión para que la otra persona haga lo que dice, aunque sabemos que fracasará)*

To drown out the noise – para mater el ruido *(ahora el ruido)*

Mary couldn't take it anymore – Mary ya no pudo soportarlo.

Hey, turn off the sink – Hey, Cierra la llave del fregadero.

Gossipy neighbor

Charlotte: I don't like to gossip, but I've heard that Joe has a new girlfriend.

Francine: Really?

Charlotte: Yes. Pauline has seen him with her several times now.

Francine: Do you think they'll get married?

Charlotte: I don't know. But you might not have a quiet bachelor for a neighbor anymore.

Francine: Do you believe everything Pauline says?

Charlotte: Why not?

Francine: She told me something about you the other day, but I don't believe her.

Charlotte: I don't either. . . . Um, so, what did she say?

Francine: About what?

Charlotte: What did she say about me?

Francine: Who?

Charlotte: Pauline!

Francine: Oh, you know Pauline. She always makes up interesting stories.

Charlotte: Interesting? What did she say about me?

Francine: Oh, nothing much. . . .Oh Look, who's this?

A car pulls up in front of the neighbor's house playing loud music. A young woman steps out and goes up to the door. She knocks. Joe walks out, and they both get in the car and drive off together.

Francine: Maybe Pauline's right.

Charlotte: You should tell me what Pauline said.

Francine: No, she wouldn't like it.

Charlotte: You know, she told me a couple things about you, too.

Francine: Really?

Charlotte: Yeah, but I probably shouldn't tell you.

Francine: Why not?

Charlotte: Well, you know, she told me in confidence.

Francine: But if it's a secret about me . . .

Charlotte: Tell you what, you tell me what she said about me, and I'll tell you what she said about you.

Francine: Ahhh, you just want to know what she said about you.

Charlotte: Don't you want to know?

Francine: Well, yes. Okay. You first.

Charlotte: No, you first.

Francine: No—Oh, okay. She told me—you won't be angry?

Charlotte: No. Well, I won't be angry at you.

Francine: She told me you have a son nobody knows about.

Charlotte: I don't have any children! I've told her I never even had an official boyfriend.

Francine: Well, I wouldn't worry about it. So, what did she say about me?

Charlotte: She said you talk about all the neighbors.

Francine: Me? You know I would never gossip.

Charlotte: Right.

Francine: I mean, I don't talk as much as Pauline.

Charlotte: Of course not. And since I'm busier

than both of you, I don't have time to stand around and talk.

Francine: What do you have to do now?

Charlotte: Well, I need to go see a friend.

Francine: A friend?

Charlotte: Yes. Um, she's not feeling well, and she asked me to . . . to, uh . . . to take her some cookies.

Francine: She needs cookies because she's not feeling well.

Charlotte: Uh, yeah.

Francine: If it's Pauline, tell her I have a great story about her.

Phrases and Expressions

Gossipy neighbor – Vecina chismosa

An official boyfriend – un novio oficial

you talk about all the neighbors – hablas de todos los vecinos.

To stand around and talk – estar por ahi y hablar.

A car breaks down on a road trip. The man tries to play the mechanic ...

It was a long weekend. On Friday night, Olivia and Jarold made lasagna and watched a movie. On Saturday, they cleaned the house and the garage. On Sunday afternoon, they were bored. They talked about doing exercise, writing a book, and putting a puzzle together. But they finally decided to go for a drive.

It was a beautiful day for a drive. It was fall. There

was a nice cool breeze and that natural fall smell in the air. The hills were covered with colorful leaves. They drove past the mall, past the outlets, past the baseball stadium, past the new high school. There were fewer buildings, more trees. They were so glad to be out in nature. Then they noticed a new smell: smoke.

They pulled over to the side of the road and stopped the car.

"It must have overheated," said Olivia.

"Let me check," said Jarold. He opened the hood of the car and stood back while steam blew everywhere. The engine was very hot. He took caps off and put them back on. Everything looked okay, except for the smoke and steam.

"Have you checked the antifreeze?" Olivia asked?

"No, I think it's fine. I'm going to add some more oil." Jarold got some oil out of the trunk and added a quart. He started up the car. The hot engine warning light was still on.

He started to remove pieces from the engine. Olivia asked him what he was doing. He was going to clean the jack valve. "Did you check the antifreeze?" she asked.

"Yes, but I can't see how high the antifreeze is."

"Have you ever cleaned the jack valve before?"

"Yes, I have—several times."

"Okay," Olivia said, and she got back in the car. She tried to work on a word puzzle, but she couldn't concentrate. She got out her cell phone and started killing little creatures that ran around in circles.

Finally, Jarold finished cleaning the jack valve. He

started the engine. It was cooler this time. They turned around and drove back for five minutes, and the hot engine light came on again. "It must be the antifreeze. Why don't you add some antifreeze, Honey?" Olivia asked.

"We'll see," he said. Jarold tried a couple more things he knew how to do. It took twenty minutes, but the car was cool again. They drove ten minutes, and the car heated up again. This time, they were near a plaza. Jared found a mechanic.

The mechanic looked the car over and added some water. "You were low on antifreeze."

Jared got back in the car. He wondered if Olivia heard what the mechanic said. He hoped she wouldn't say anything. And she didn't. He tried to start the car. He was pretty sure it would be okay this time. But it wouldn't go! He looked at the indicator. The hot engine light wasn't on, but another light was. The gas tank was empty!

"Aha!" he said. "I guess it was a simple problem after all. We're out of gas."

Olivia laughed. He looked at Olivia, but she didn't look up from her game.

Phrases and Expressions

Putting a puzzle together – Armando un rompecabeza

To be out in nature – estar fuera en la naturaleza

Steam blew everywhere – humo (vapor) salia por todos lados.

He looked at the indicator – miró el indicador

We're out of gas – nos quedamos sin combustible.

Booking a hotel room

A middle-aged man walks into a hotel out of the rain and stands in front of the front desk. The clerk is on the phone. "Yes, she did! I heard her. She said that her boyfriend is"— The clerk turns and sees the client and continues, "staying in room 42B. Yes, I'll be sure to tell him."

"How can I help you?" she asked the man.

"Hi. I'd like a room."

"Of course. Double bed?"

"Two."

"Two double beds?"

"Yes."

"Smoking or non?"

"Nonsmoking."

"Fine." She makes a quick call. "If you'll just wait a couple minutes."

"What am I waiting for?"

"The room."

"It's not ready?"

"Well, we're getting it ready for you right now."

The man goes out to the car and comes back with his wife and daughter and the suitcases. They sit down to wait. He asks for a magazine. The clerk hands him a celebrity magazine and a cooking magazine. Five minutes go by. He asks about the room.

"If you'd like one queen bed, I have a room ready right now," she tells him.

He says he can wait. After ten minutes, the clerk

gives him his keycard and tells him where his room is. But when they find the room, there are just a couples sheets on the beds, the bathroom has hair on the floor, and there is no refrigerator. He goes back to the front desk.

"I expected the room to be a little bit cleaner," he tells the clerk. "In fact, the room isn't at all what I was expecting."

She comes to see the room. She takes some toilet paper and uses it to pick up the hair. She offers to put their food in the staff refrigerator overnight and promises to bring some blankets. "Will that be all?" she asks when she returns.

"Do you have room service?" he asks.

"We do have room service until 10, but that's closed now. There's a vending machine down the hall with an ice machine and a washing machine."

"What about coffee? Can I get some coffee? I expected the room to have a coffee pot."

She promises to bring him a cup of coffee. While she is gone, he starts to take a shower, but he notices that water is dripping from the light bulb over the shower. He complains to the clerk.

"I'm sorry," she says. "Would you like another room?"

He agrees, but she tells him it will be another ten or fifteen minutes. When they finally get their new room, they notice it smells like smoke. The clerk apologizes but says it's the only room left.

The man says, "I'm really disappointed in this hotel. It's supposed to be a five-star hotel! Who gave this place its rating?"

"Oh, no, sir. This isn't rated a five-star hotel. That's the name of the hotel: Five Stars."

Phrases and Expressions

A middle-aged man – un hombre de mediana edad

Water is dripping from the light bulb – el agua esta goteando del bombillo

I'm really disappointed – estoy realmente decepcionado

Who gave this place its rating? – ¿quién dio la calificación a este lugar?

This isn't rated a five-star hotel – no esta calificado como un hotel cinco estrella.

That's the name of the hotel: Five Stars – ese es el nombre del hotel: Cinco Estrellas.

Reporting little Charlie

A man went up to a police officer and asked for help. "What can I do for you?" the officer asked.

"I've lost little Charlie," he replied with tears in his eyes.

"Missing person," said the police officer as he opened a notebook. "Can you describe Charlie?"

"Yes, he's short and muscular."

"Muscular?"

"Yes, he's very strong. You should see him run!"

"Okay. How old is he?" asked the policeman.

"He's almost three."

"Two. What color are his eyes and hair?"

"He has brown eyes, brown hair."

"What about his skin color—light or dark?"

"Um, I don't know," replied the man. "Dark, I guess."

The policeman stared at him. "Okay. What clothes is he wearing?"

"Clothes? He's not wearing any clothes."

"Just a diaper?"

"No. nothing. I know some people get them clothes and everything, but I think that's a waste of money."

The policeman looked surprised. He was beginning to think this man was probably very negligent with his little boy. "When did you last see him?" he asked.

"Well, you see, we were playing ball. And I threw it pretty far. He went running after the ball, and he didn't come back."

"How long ago was this?"

"Maybe ten minutes," answered the man. When he saw a look of disapprobation on the police officer's face, he explained, "I've looked everywhere for him."

"Are there any other unique identifiers you can think of—eyeglasses and such?"

The man seemed to think that was funny and said he couldn't think of anything unique except that he had pointed ears.

"Pointed ears?" repeated the policeman. "That's unusual."

The man said that it was actually quite common. The policeman was thinking that this man was really strange.

"And he's ugly," the man added. The policeman's

mouth feel open. He couldn't believe anyone would talk about their child that way. "Really," the man insisted. "He's very ugly. You know, he has spikey hair and all."

"Wow. Um, we'll get a couple officers on it as soon as we can. Meanwhile, you keep looking for him. Call to him, anything you can think of."

"Okay, thank you so much, Officer."

The policeman walked over into the shade and made a call to headquarters to report the missing child. When he finished, he joined the man to help him look. He found the man calling to Charlie.

"Here, Charlie, Charlie,"

"Is that how you normally call your son?" the officer asked.

"Oh, he's not my son. We adopted him."

"But still," argued the police officer, "that's not a very dignified way to refer to a little boy."

"Well, he's not a little boy."

"What is he?"

"He's a dog—a Peruvian Inca Orchid, actually, a very expensive breed."

The policeman sighed. "Uh, Sir. I'm sorry. But we can't help you look for a dog. We can only help in the case of missing persons. I'm going to have to cancel the report. But best of luck to you. I hope you find him soon, and if I see him, I'll be sure to let you know."

Phrases and Expressions
With tears in his eyes – con lagrimas en sus ojos
Missing person – persona desaparecida

he's short and muscular – él es bajito y musculoso

That's a waste of money – es una perdida de dinero

Very negligent with his little boy – muy negligente con su pequeño hijo.

He had pointed ears – tiene orejas puntiagudas

That's not a very dignified way – esa no es una forma digna

Surprise

A young man wearing a ski mask and and swimming trunks forced open a screen door on a nice home in the suburbs. He found himself surrounded by violets, doilies, and family portraits. Well, he knew this was an old lady's house and that he probably wouldn't find a lot of electronics, but there would be jewelry and maybe even money stashed somewhere.

When he walked into the kitchen, he was surprised to find a smartphone charging on the counter. "Nice!" he said under his breath. He was hungry, so he checked the fridge. Steak! He got some out and ate as he checked out the phone's features. The sink was empty. He washed his dishes. "Don't want to leave any evidence," he thought.

Then he headed into the living room. The TV console was ancient—vintage, actually. It even had a dial! He turned it on. The picture quality wasn't bad. There was a black-and-white program on. He felt as if he had gone back in time. He took a selfie with the new phone on the old sofa, with the doiles, watching vintage TV. He felt tired after eating the steak, and he soon fell asleep.

Suddenly, he woke up with the feeling that someone was watching him. A sweet little old lady with curlers in her hair was staring at him. She looked very entertained.

The burglar felt irritated at her for laughing at him.

"Now, listen, Ma'am. You're going to sit on the couch. I'll just take a few things and go away."

"You want to bet?" replied the old lady.

"Don't make a noise and don't even think of calling the police until I'm gone. I don't want to hurt you. Just sit down and calm down, and nothing will happen to you."

"No, nothing will happen to me. But you'll be surprised at what is going to happen to you!" She kicked him as he started to stand up. He tried to grab her, but she whirled around and kicked him again. He couldn't believe his eyes. She was a karate expert. What luck! Of all the houses on the block, he had to choose the one with a grandma karate champion.

He said, "Okay. I won't take anything else. I'll let you go easy. I'll just leave now."

"No, you won't," she said. "Where's my cell phone?"

He slowly took the cell phone out of his pocket and handed it to her. Then he started toward the door. She jumped in front of him. "What about the kitchen?" she demanded. "You got the floor all dirty. Get in there and clean it up."

Before he knew it, he was on his hands and knees scrubbing the floor with a rag. He'd never done this before, and he was disgusted by the hair on his hands.

When the floor looked pretty good, he asked, "Can I go now?" His tone of voice was much more respectful than when he saw the lady for the first time.

"You can go," she said. Then she showed him her cell phone. "I hope you've learned your lesson. But I've already uploaded this picture, and if you ever come back, I'll share it on my social network!"

Phrases and Expressions

Swimming trunks – traje de baño

Forced open a screen door – Abrió a la fuerza una puerta de tela metálica

An old lady's house – la casa de una anciana

Money stashed somewhere – dinero escondido en algún lugar

Don't want to leave any evidence – no quiero dejar evidencia

The burglar felt irritated – el ladrón se enojó

You want to bet? – ¿quieres apostarlo?

Grandma karate champion – Abuela campeona de karate

I'll let you go easy – te dejaré ir fácil (sin problemas)

Level Two Tests – Examenes del Nivel Dos

Estos son los exámenes para pasar el nivel dos. Asegúrense de tomar su tiempo y completarlos correctamente. Una vez los hayan completado y estén completamente seguros que han terminado. Pueden presentarlos a un amigo de habla inglesa para que los revise y les diga si lo hicieron bien, o pueden enviarme un email con sus exámenes. Sin en algún punto, aun están dudosos, deberán repasarlo y asegurarse de dominarlo muy bien. El segundo nivel es esencial para todo el aprendizaje, sin dominarlo bien, no podremos aprender bien. Es imperativo dominar a la perfección cada uno de los conceptos presentados en este nivel. ***Good luck once again!***

Test Level exams – Test 5 covers units 1 to 3.

Test 1.1: Adjectives and Adverbs—write the correct form of the word.

Example: She got up and _noisily_ walked to the bathroom. (noisy)

1. The _____ boy left the door open. (careless)
2. The baby's mom _____ closed the door. (quiet)
3. You have worked really _____. (hard)

4. That is a really _____ truck! (fast)
5. He was tired, and he worked very

_____. (slow)

6.   I was so _____ when I found the cake! (happy)

7.   I had a _____ day! (bad)

8.   My pillow is so _____. (soft)

Test 1.2: Put the words in the correct spaces.

ahead   corner   turn

Go straight (1) _____. Then (2) _____

left at the (3) _____.

across   down   over

The store is on the other side of the street. It's (4)

_____ the street.

A bird flew (5) _____ the house.

Grandma walks (6) _____ the street to visit her friend.

Test 1.3: What comes next? Write the letter of a logical statement to come next.

1.   _____ If you like the TV program,

2.   _____I used to play with blocks.

3.   _____   Would you like a flower?

a.   I have lots of them, and they are so beautiful.

b.   You can watch it tomorrow, too!

c.   Now I work all the time.

Test 1.4: Make the questions more polite. Make indirect questions.

Example: What day is today?   Could you tell me _what day today is?_

1.   Can I use the phone?   Do you mind if

_____

2.   Why are you sad?   May   I   ask

_____

3.   Where is the museum?   Do   you   know

_____

4.   How is everyone getting to the party?   Could you tell me _____

Test 6 covers units 4-6.

Test 6.1: Agree with everything (*so* or *too/neither* or *either*).

Example: I shouldn't stay up too late. _Neither should I. OR I shouldn't either._

1.   I am always in a good mood.

_____

2.   I can't stand milk.

_____

3.   I should go home now.

_____

4. I won't go to the funeral.

_____

5. I haven't studied for the test!

_____

6. I've eaten a whole pizza!

_____

7. I'll give $200 to charity.

_____

8. I can swim faster than a goldfish.

_____

9. I'm not very happy

_____

10. I shouldn't eat a lot of bread.

_____

Test 6.2: You are always superior. Use the comparative to say you are better at everything.
Example: Jane can run very fast.   _I can run faster than Jane._

1. Mark is really tall.

    _____

2. My dad is so funny.

    _____

3. Our teacher is really intelligent.

    _____

4. Yikes. That frog is really ugly.

    _____

5. My boyfriend studies all the time.

    _____

Test 6.3: Check [✓] if they mean the same thing. Do nothing if they mean something different.

1. ❑   This is terrible! You should be doing your homework. / You will be doing your homework.

2. ❑   I would go with you. / I will go with you.

3. ❑   Could you help me? / Would you help me?

4. ❑   They should eat first. / They will eat first.

5. ❑   She shouldn't pick up her toys. / She won't pick up her toys.

6. ❑   They should arrive tomorrow. / They will arrive tomorrow.

7. ❑   My mom? Hmm. Right now, she'll be at

home right now. / Right now, she should be at home.

8. ❑   I will help you! / I should help you!

9. ❑   They should have asked permission. / They will have asked permission.

10. ❑   Let's see, it's 5 p.m. She must be on her way here. / She should be on her way here.

11. ❑   Do you want me to call your mom? / Would you like me to call your mom?

12. ❑   Should you open the door, please? / Will you open the door, please?

Test 7.1: Circle the letter of the best response.

1.   Achoo! [sneeze]
a.   Congratulations!
b.   Bless you!
c.   Thank you!

2.   Why don't you work for Fran Friday night?
a.   I can't. I have a dentist appointment.
b.   I would do it, but I already have plans.
c.   I could, but she hasn't asked me.
d.   All are grammatical responses.

3.   I'm going to be busy next week.
a.   I can't either.
b.   You're crazy.
c.   Neither is Mom.
d.   So am I.

4.   Have you ever been to the Grand Canyon?
a.   Yes. I've been there three times.
b.   I went last year.
c.   Never.
d.   All are grammatical responses.

5.   Could you help me with my homework?
a.   Let's go next week.

 b. Why don't you do it now?

 c. I'd like to, but I'm really busy.

 d. Yes, I'd like some.

 6. Are you doing okay?

 a. I think yes.

 b. I guess so.

 c. I hope not.

 d. I yes, really.

 7. What did you use to do before you met your wife?

 a. I went hunting once.

 b. I always clean the house.

 c. I always played video games.

 d. All are logical responses.

 8. Would you like to go to the zoo?

 a. Right now? Let's go!

 b. We often go to the zoo.

 c. Mom loves the zoo.

 d. I haven't seen that one.

Test 7.2: Underline the correct word or phrase in parentheses.

 1. The Amazon River is (**longer / the longest**) river in the world!

 2. If I finish my homework in time, I (**will / should**) help you.

 3. Unfortunately, they are (**taller / the tallest**) than me.

 4. I haven't (**ate / eaten**) dinner.

 5. My brother is (**taller/ the tallest**) than my dad.

 6. Don't give up! I (**am going to / will**) help you.

 7. Have you (**saw / seen**) the new cartoon?

 8. I've felt bad (**since / before**) I ate the shrimp

cocktail.

9. I'm as slow (**as / to**) a sloth.

10. Mom, you just (**will / have to**) come. It's going to be great!

Test 7.3: Write the correct word: *in, off, on, out, up, to.*

Example: I didn't get _____ the store on time. It's closed.

1. Don't forget to check _____ to the hotel before you eat.

2. You have to get _____ early if you want to be successful.

3. Her flight takes _____ at 6 a.m.

4. We're going to eat _____ for her birthday.

5. Put _____ your sweater. It's cold outside.

6.

Verb list – Lista de verbos

To answer the phone – contestar el teléfono

To apologize – ofrecer disculpas, disculparse

To ask – pedir / preguntar

To be a pain in the neck – ser un fastidio

To be in love – estar enamorado

To be right – estar en lo cierto (correcto) / tener la razón

To be robbed – ser robado

To be shot – ser baleado / recibir un tiro.

To be wrong – estar equivocado

To become - convertirse

To believe - creer

To borrow – tomar prestado (se toma prestado algo de alguien)

To breathe - respirar

To brush - cepillar

To call – llamar

To carry – cargar / llevar

To catch – atrapar / agarrar

To change - cambiar

To check in - registrarse

To choose – elegir / escoger

To chuckle - reír

To clean - limpiar

To close - cerrar

To comb – peinarse

To come right in – entrar de inmediato (cuando la persona está dentro y te invita a entrar)

To compare - comparar

To describe – describir

To dial – marcar

To do the housework – hacer los deberes de la casa

To do the laundry – lavar la ropa

To do your best – hacer lo mejor, dar tu mejor esfuerzo

To do your homework – hacer la tarea

To dust - despolvar

To eat out – comer fuera (un restaurante, etc)

To examine - examinar

To exchange – intercambiar

To find out – descubrir

To fly – volar

To forget – olvidar

To get a disease – contraer una enfermedad

To get a haircut – recortarse el pelo

To get a job – conseguir un trabajo / empleo.

To get a shave - afeitarse

To get sick - enfermarse

To get to – llegar a (un lugar o destino)

To get well - mejorarse

To go dancing – salir a bailar

To go for a drive – dar un paseo en vehículo

To go for a meal – salir a comer

To go for a swim – salir a nadar

To go for a walk – salir a caminar

To go in – entrar (cuando la persona está afuera y va a entrar)

To go right in – entrar de inmediato (cuando la persona está afuera y te indica que entres)

To hang up – colgar

To happen – suceder / ocurrir / pasar

To have a look at – dar una mirada (ojeada)

To have an operation - operarse

To have something ready – tener algo listo

To have your hands full – tener las manos llenas
To hit – golpear
To hurt – lastimar / doler
To invite – invitar
To iron – planchar
To jump – saltar / brincar
To keep an eye on activity - vigilar la actividades
To kill – matar
To know why – saber el por qué
To land – aterrizar
To last – durar / perdurar
To lend – prestar (se presta algo a alguien)
To lie – yacer / tenderse
To lie down – recostarse
To look – mirar / observar
To look after – cuidar
To look like – parecerse / ser similar
To lose weight – perder peso
To make a mistake – cometer un error / meter la pata
To miss – extrañar / faltar / errar
To mop - trapear
To pick up – recoger
To promised – prometer
To put on weight – subir de peso
To rave about it – alardear a cerca de algo
To refuse – rehúsar
To remember – recordar
To rent – rentar
To ride – montar (bicicleta, caballo, etc.)
To ring – sonar
To shave – afeitar

To shout – gritar / vocear / vociferar

To sign – firmar

To smell – oler

To sneeze – estornudar

To steal – robar / hurtar

To sweep - barrer

To take a vacation – tomar vacaciones

To take off – despegar / quitarse

To take someone's temperature – tomar la temperatura de alguien

To take the bus – tomar el autobús (abordarlo)

To take the plane – tomar al avión (abordarlo)

To taste – probar / saborear

To thank – agradecer

To throw – arrojar / lanzar

To turn – girar / voltear

To turn down – bajar el volumen

To turn up – subir el volumen

To understand why – entender el por qué

To use – usar

To visit – visitar

To wake up –despertarse

To wear – usar

To weigh – pesar

Grammar Summary

Lesson One

Tag questions – Coletilla interrogativa

Would (wouldn't) like – Gustaría (no)

Adjectives – Adjetivos

Adverbs – Adverbios

New regular verbs – Nuevos verbos regulares

New irregular verbs – Nuevos verbos irregulares

Lesson Two

"could you tell… May I ask…"

Modal verb Can / Could – Verbo modal Can / Could.

Auxiliary verb "used to" – Verbo auxiliar"used to" – solía.

New regular verbs – Nuevos verbos regulares

New irregular verbs – Nuevos verbos irregulares

Prepositions – Preposiciones

Adjectives – Adjetivos

Adverbs – Adverbios

The word "so" – La palabra "so"

Lesson Three

Pronouns in affirmative sentences – Pronombres en oraciones afirmativas.

Pronouns in interrogative sentences – pronombres en oraciones interrogativas

Pronouns in negative sentences – Pronombres en

oraciones negativas

Relative pronouns as a subject "Who / That" – Pronombres relativos como sujeto "Who / That".

Question words plus infinitive / Present progressive – Palabras interrogativas más el infinitivo / Presente progresivo.

Conjunctions – Conjunciones

Pronouns and adjectives – Pronombres and adjetivos.

Regular verbs – Verbos regulares

Irregular verbs – Verbos irregulares

Adverbs - Adverbios

Adjectives – Adjetivos

Lesson Four

Present perfect tense – Tiempo presente perfecto.

Structure of the Present perfect – Estructura del presente perfecto.

Past participle – Pasado participio

Have to – tener que

Adverbs – Adverbios

Adjectives – Adjetivos

Lesson Five

Would - condicional

Comparing people and things with adjectives – Comparando personas y cosas con adjetivos.

Superlative – Superlativo

Irregular superlatives – Superlativos irregulares

Auxiliary verb "must" – Verbo auxiliar "must".

Adjectives – Adjetivos

Prepositions – Preposiciones

Nivel Dos

New regular verbos – Nuevos verbos regulares
New irregular verbs – Nuevos verbos irregulares

Lesson Six

The future with "Will" – El futuro con "Wll"
Polite commands – Órdenes o mandatos de cortesía.
The auxiliary verb "Should" – El verbo auxiliar "Should".
The verb "to get" – El Verbo "to get".
Adjectives "no / any" and Pronouns "None / Any" – Adjetivos "no / any" y Pronombres "none / any".
Conjunctions – Conjunciones
Adjectives – Adjetivos
Adverbs – Adverbios
New regular verbs – Nuevos verbos regulares
New irregular verbs – Nuevos verbos irregulares

Answers to exercises – Respuestas de los ejercicios

Como terminaron sus exámenes y se aseguraron de dominar cada concepto, pueden verificar las respuestas al final del libro. Me he tomado la libertad de ofrecerles las respuestas de todos los ejercicios de cada lección asi también como los del examen de nivel. Pero no hagan trampa, solo ustedes pierden si hacen trampa. *See you on the third volume.*

Lesson One

Answers to Exercise 1.1:

1. isn't she?
2. did it?
3. don't you?
4. isn't she?
5. was he?
6. can you?
7. does she?
8. can't you?
9. is he?
10. don't you?

Answers to Exercise 1.2:

1. If she wants to get her work done, she shouldn't watch soap operas.
2. If they want to make extra money, they can deliver newspapers.
3. If Mom lets you go to the movies, call me first!
4. If you finish your work early, we can go out to eat!
5. If it rains, I can't do the laundry.

Answers to Exercise 1.3:

1. How many

2. Which
3. When
4. Why
5. Where

Lesson Two
Answers to Exercise 2.1:
1. tourist (person, not place)
2. jail (place—noun, not verb)
3. noisily (adverb, not adjective)
4. ground (place, not direction)
5. band (group, not person)

Answers to Exercise 2.2:
1. say
2. spoke
3. understand
4. paid
5. looked
6. could
7. got
8. was
9. sat
10. saw
11. cried

Answers to Exercise 2.3:
1. The guest noisily walked down the hall.
2. The groom quickly kissed the bride.
3. He quietly left the boring class.
4. They happily paid for the gold rings.
5. The artist's studio is across the hall.

Answers to Exercise 2.4:

1. Can you tell me where the restroom is? / May I ask where the restroom is?
2. May I ask what your name is?
3. May I ask where you are from?
4. Can you tell me when the movie starts? / May I ask when the movie starts?
5. Can you tell me where the museum is? / May I ask where the museum is?

Lesson Three
Answers to Exercise 3.1:

1. Another
2. Each other
3. The other
4. Another
5. The other

Answers to Exercise 3.2:

1. Do you know why the bank is closed?
2. Do you know how I can rent a boat?
3. Do you know when the boat comes back?
4. Do you know where the other boats are?
5. Do you know who the manager is?

Answers to Exercise 3.3:

1. I know where it is.
2. I know when it starts.
3. I know what to do.
4. I know who he is calling.
5. I know where she is going.

Answers to Exercise 3.4:

1. anything
2. Nobody
3. something
4. anyone
5. Everyone

Lesson Four
Answers to Exercise 4.1:
1. Have, had
2. have, looked
3. 've ruined
4. have sold
5. 've seen
6. Have, been
7. 've, tried
8. have, worn
9. Have, flown
10. have fixed

Answers to Exercise 4.2
1. haircut
2. housework
3. homework
4. swim
5. drive

Answers to Exercise 4.3:
1. ever
2. already
3. never
4. just
5. yet

Lesson Five
Answers to Exercise 5.1:
1. It's 5:45. You must leave now if you want to catch the bus.
2. I can't say no. My country needs me. I must go.
3. Dan didn't come to work today. He must be sick.
4. But, Mom, just look at all that snow! Do I have to **shovel** the sidewalk?
5. Ingrid looks pretty happy. She must have finished her project.

Answers to Exercise 5.2:
1. I am shorter than John.
2. Chocolate chips cost more than chocolate bars.
3. My boyfriend is the smartest one in the class.
4. Our house is the ugliest house on the block.
5. It's dryer outside than inside.

Answers to Exercise 5.3:
1. c
2. e
3. a
4. f
5. d
6. b

Lesson Six
Answers to Exercise 6.1:
1. There isn't any more.

2. There aren't any more.
3. There aren't any more.
4. There isn't any more.
5. There aren't any more.

Answers to Exercise 6.2:
1. I can, too. / So can I.
2. I should, too. / So should I.
3. I was, too. / So was I.
4. I didn't either. / Neither did I.
5. I will, too. / So will I.

Answers to Exercise 6.3:
1. I want you to do your homework.
2. Can you send me the file again, please?
3. Can I have some juice?
4. Could you sign here, please?
5. Don't open the door.

Answers to Level Two Tests – Respuesta de los Examenes del Nivel Dos

Answers to Test 1.1:
1. careless (adj.)
2. quietly (adv.—¿cómo cerró la puerta?)
3. hard (adv. sin cambio de forma—¿cómo trabajó?)
4. fast (adj.)
5. slowly (adv.—¿cómo trabajó?)
6. happy (adj.)
7. bad (adj.)
8. soft (adj.)

Answers to Test 1.2:
1. ahead
2. turn
3. corner
4. across
5. over
6. down

Answers to Test 1.3:
1. B
2. C
3. A

Answers to Test 1.4:
1. I use the phone?
2. why you are sad?
3. where the museum is?
4. how everyone is getting to the party?

Answers to Test 6.1:

1. So am I. / I am, too.
2. I can't either. / Neither can I.
3. I should, too. / So should I.
4. I won't either. / Neither will I.
5. I haven't either. Neither have I.
6. I have, too. / So have I.
7. I will, too. / So will I.
8. I can, too. / So can I.
9. I'm not either. / Neither am I.
10. I shouldn't either. / Neither should I.

Answers to Test 6.2:

1. I am taller than Mark.
2. I'm funnier than your dad.
3. I'm more intelligent than your teacher.
4. I'm uglier than that frog.
5. I study more than your boyfriend.

Answers to Test 6.3:

1. ❏ *Should* shows advice or obligation; *will* shows a prediction or order for the future.
2. ❏ *Would* shows a desire or wish; *will* gives an offer or promise.
3. ☑ They both politely ask for help.
4. ❏ *Should* gives advice; *will* gives a prediction.
5. ❏ *Should* gives advice; *will* shows her refusal to do something.
6. ❏ *Should* gives a probability; *will* gives a more sure prediction.
7. ☑ Both are guesses/assumptions based on habits.

8. ❏ *Will* gives an offer; *should* shows a feeling of responsibility.

9. ❏ *Should* shows a feeling of guilt; *will* gives a probability in the past.

10. ☑ Both make a prediction, although *must* is stronger than *should*.

11. ☑ Both politely offer to do something.

12. ❏ *Should* makes no sense *(no se puede)*; *will* asks for help.

Answers to Test 7.1:

1. B
2. D
3. D
4. D
5. C
6. B
7. C
8. A

Answers to Test 7.2:

1. the longest
2. will
3. taller
4. eaten
5. taller
6. will
7. seen
8. since
9. as
10. have to

Conclusión

Muchas gracias por seleccionar el *Curso Completo de Inglés – Nivel Dos* por Yeral E. Ogando para su aprendizaje. Por fin, han llegado al final del segundo nivel, por lo tanto, ya pueden hablar inglés fluido y están listos para el nivel tres.

Les exhorto que continúen practicando y hablando inglés en todo momento, ya les he dicho que la Practica hace al Maestro. Visiten mi pagina de internet para más información.

God bless you and see you in volumen three.

Dr. Yeral E.Ogando
www.aprendeis.com

BONO GRATIS

Estimado Estudiante,

Necesitas descargar el audio MP3 para usar este increíble método para aprender inglés. Visita este link: http://aprendeis.com/ingles-audio-nivel2/
Usuario "ennivel2"
Contraseña "en22016"

Solo tienes que descargar el archivo comprimido, descomprimirlo y estas listo para iniciar tu experiencia al mundo del inglés.

Si quieres compartir tu experiencia, comentario o possible sugerencia, siempre podrás contactarme a info@aprendeis.com

Muchas gracias por estudiar el *Curso Completo de Inglés – Nivel Dos* y por escuchar mis instrucciones.

Caros afectos,
Dr. Yeral E. Ogando

Otros libros escritos por Yeral E. Ogando

Conciencia: El Héroe Dentro de Ti

Curso Completo de Inglés – Nivel Uno

Yeral E. Ogando Proviene de un origen muy
humilde y continúa siendo un humilde siervo de
nuestro Señor Todopoderoso; entendiendo que no
somos más que recipientes y el Señor nos llama y nos
envía también a hacer Su trabajo, no nuestro trabajo.
Lucas 17:10 "Así también vosotros, cuando hayáis
hecho todo lo que os ha sido ordenado, decid: Siervos

inútiles somos, pues lo que debíamos hacer, hicimos".

El Señor Ogando nació en el Caribe, República Dominicana. Es el padre amado de dos bellas chicas Yeiris y Tiffany.

Jesús le trajo a Sus pies en la edad de 16-17 años. Desde entonces, ha servido como Co-pastor, Pastor, profesor de la Biblia en las escuelas, consejero de jóvenes, plantador y fundador de iglesias. Actualmente está sirviendo como Secretario para la Iglesia Reformada Dominicana así como de enlace para Haití y EE.UU.

Fluido en varias lenguas el Señor Ogando es el Creador y dueño de un Ministerio de Traducción On-line que opera desde el 2007; con traductores cristianos Nativos en más de 25 países.

(www.christian-translation.com),

Lo más apasionante acerca de su Ministerio de Traducción es que miles de personas están recibiendo la Palabra de Dios en su lengua nativa diariamente y cientos de ministerios logran llegar al mundo a través del trabajo de Christian-translation.com junto con su red de traducción de 17 sitios web relacionados con traducciones cristianas, a diferentes lenguas.

www.ingramcontent.com/pod-product-compliance
Lightning Source LLC
Chambersburg PA
CBHW031547040426
42452CB00006B/230